A REPUBLIC OF PARTIES?

Enduring Questions in American Political Life
Series Editor: Wilson Carey McWilliams, Rutgers University

This series explores the political, social, and cultural issues that originated during the founding of the American nation but are still heatedly debated today. Each book offers teachers and students a concise but comprehensive summary of the issue's evolution, along with the crucial documents spanning the range of American history. In addition, *Enduring Questions in American Political Life* provides insightful contemporary perspectives that illuminate the enduring relevance and future prospects of important issues on the American political landscape.

The Choice of the People? Debating the Electoral College
    Judith A. Best, foreword by Thomas E. Cronin
A Wall of Separation? Debating the Public Role of Religion
    Mary C. Segers and Ted G. Jelen, introduction by Clarke E. Cochran
A Republic of Parties? Debating the Two-Party System
    Theodore J. Lowi and Joseph Romance, introduction by Gerald M. Pomper

A REPUBLIC OF PARTIES?

Debating the Two-Party System

Theodore J. Lowi
and Joseph Romance

Introduction by Gerald M. Pomper

ROWMAN & LITTLEFIELD PUBLISHERS, INC.
Lanham • Boulder • New York • Oxford

ROWMAN & LITTLEFIELD PUBLISHERS, INC.

Published in the United States of America
by Rowman & Littlefield Publishers, Inc.
4720 Boston Way, Lanham, Maryland 20706

12 Hid's Copse Road
Cumnor Hill, Oxford OX2 9JJ, England

British Library Cataloguing in Publication Information Available

Library of Congress Cataloging-in-Publication Data

Lowi, Theodore J.
    A republic of parties? : debating the two-party system / by
Theodore J. Lowi and Joseph Romance.
        p.   cm.—(Enduring questions in American political life)
    Includes bibliographical references and index.
    ISBN 0-8476-8608-6 (hardcover : alk. paper).—ISBN 0-8476-8609-4
(pbk. : alk. paper)
    1. Political parties—United States.   2. Third parties (United
States politics).   3. Political parties—United States—History—
Sources.   4. Third parties (United States politics)—History—
Sources.   I. Romance, Joseph, 1966– . II. Title. III. Series.
JK2261.L68   1998
324.73—DC21   98-24980
                                                                        CIP

Printed in the United States of America

⊚ ™ The paper used in this publication meets the minimum requirements of
American National Standard for Information Sciences—Permanence of Paper for
Printed Library Materials, ANSI Z39.48-1984.

Contents

Introduction

The Place of American Political Parties

Gerald M. Pomper

A generation ago, a leading scholar began a book on American politics with these axioms: "No America without democracy, no democracy without politics, no politics without parties, no parties without compromise and moderation."[1]

By the 1990s, two modern writers would consider parties less important, predicting, "[It] seems unlikely that the parties can reverse the events that have made them the servants rather than the masters of successful independent politicians,"[2] and a noted analyst deplored "a destructive interest-group entrenchment in Washington and loss of vitality in the nation's two-party system."[3]

Yet, even while acknowledging these changes and problems, the keenest contemporary scholar of parties would return to the earlier assertions in concluding his own book: "In America, democracy is unthinkable save in terms of a two-party system, because no collection of ambitious politicians has long been able to think of a way to achieve their goals in this democracy save in terms of political parties."[4]

As evident in these statements, political parties foster disagreement about both their normative value and their empirical reality. American history and practice shows similar uncertainties. We disliked political parties even before we were a true nation: James Madison urged the adoption of the Constitution as a safeguard against the "mischief of faction." That distrust continues to the present: a majority of voters prefer that Congress and the presidency be controlled by different parties.

In practice, America developed the world's first democratic political parties soon after the adoption of the Constitution—with Madison himself in the lead. Yet the decline of parties has been regularly announced and advocated. By 1835, Alexis de Tocqueville declared that "Great political parties, then, are

not to be met with in the United States at the present time. . . . In the absence
of great parties the United States swarms with lesser controversies. . . . The
pains that are taken to create parties are inconceivable, and at the present day
it is no easy task."[5]

At the end of the nineteenth century, another distinguished observer, Mosei
Ostrogorski, acknowledged that party loyalty "filled a portion of the moral
void; it met an emotional need." But he also happily believed that "public
morality has advanced. . . . Public opinion is beginning to extricate itself from
the narrow and deadly groove of parties."[6] By our time, the end of the twentieth century, Ross Perot and the Reform Party also expected the end of the
contemporary party system, urged on in this volume by Theodore Lowi.

The American aversion to political parties can be seen in the current controversy over campaign finance reform. Record spending on the 1996 campaigns
has led to widespread criticism, elaborate investigations in both houses of
Congress as well as the Department of Justice, and late-night comedy routines
about President Clinton's courting of contributors with coffees at the White
House and overnight stays in the Lincoln bedroom of the executive mansion.

There certainly are serious policy questions about campaign finance, such
as the unequal access that may be bought by campaign contributors and the
way campaign costs create high barriers to political activity. What is striking
about this controversy, however, is its concentration on the practice of "soft
money," contributions to the political parties rather than to individual candidates. Congressional investigators and editorial writers seem "shocked,
shocked" that the parties use this money to support campaigns by their respective Democratic or Republican candidates. The *New York Times,* for example,
found it suspicious that President Clinton urged luncheon guests to contribute
to the Democratic Party in 1996.[7] Self-styled "reformers" disagree on many
points, but their one area of agreement is that this "soft money" should be
abolished. The argument seems to be that political money may be disreputable
generally, but it is particularly corrupt if it involves political parties.

Why? Do we regard it as strange if parents use their resources for the benefit
of their children? Would we be suspicious if Burger King subsidized the ad-
vertising of its local franchises? Would we favor legislation prohibiting major
league baseball teams from paying the salaries of the managers of their farm
teams? The difference appears to be that we look with favor on parents, corporations, and baseball, but we disapprove of political parties. This disapproval
is based on an unclear understanding of the character of political parties and
their vital role in American democracy. This volume, we may hope, will lead
to greater clarity.

Why Parties?[8]

Misunderstanding starts with the very concept of a political party. Academic
works often begin with Edmund Burke's definition of a party as "a body of

men united, for promoting by their joint endeavors . . . some particular principle in which they are all agreed."[9] When we find, as we typically do, that parties are not united or consistently principled, we come to see them as selfish, hypocritical, deceptive, and undesirable.

A better understanding would see a political party as indeed self-interested, as, to put it bluntly, "first of all an organized attempt to get power."[10] This definition not only is more accurate but also has two further advantages. First, it enables us to compare parties to other self-interested organizations, such as corporations and baseball teams. Second, it changes the standard of evaluation: we can now ask, "Do parties fulfill their social function?" not "Are parties morally good?"

Parties are best seen as groups of ambitious men and women who band together to achieve their political goals, the primary goal being power. People want power for a variety of reasons. Principles, and related public policies, are certainly one reason for seeking power, and party politicians show dedication to principles much more often and more consistently than commonly assumed. But there are other reasons for seeking power, including the material rewards of office, prestige, excitement, and social contacts. Typically, in reality, there is no direct clash between principles and power-seeking: a politician promotes his or her principles by holding power. On relatively rare occasions, there is a conflict, and politicians must make difficult choices—seeking compromise, fudging issues, waiting for a better time to push their programs, supporting a less desirable but more electable candidate, reversing course, and even abandoning their careers. The conflict between principled conscience and political ambition makes for good drama,[11] but it does not describe the ordinary world of politics.

Analytically, we do better by emphasizing parties as collective organizations of power-seekers. The politically ambitious create, join, change, and sometimes destroy parties because "rational, elective office-seekers and holders use the party to achieve their goals." Parties provide politicians with efficient channels for individual ambition; they provide a way to develop public policy from the clash of divergent interests; they provide workers, loyalties, and resources to mobilize the electorate.[12]

The parties seek power in ways similar to a corporation's search for profits and a baseball team's search for victory. All of these groups work to meet the demands of their "customers." Burger King develops a food menu that will satisfy its patrons' hunger for hamburgers and fries. The New York Yankees recruit a lineup of skilled hitters and pitchers to bring fans to the park. And the political parties provide a menu, a lineup, an agenda to win votes. But notice that all of these organizations are self-interested. They don't provide their services because they always like those who eat, cheer, and vote. They do so because their own profits, ticket sales, and election victories depend on winning the customers' approval.

As these groups pursue their self-interests, they also promote more general interests—not because they intend to, but because they must do so, in order to meet the competition. Burger King competes with McDonald's, resulting in more food choices for the consumer. The Yankees compete with twenty-nine other teams, resulting in more skillful contests. Democrats compete with Republicans, resulting in more attention to popular desires.

Parties and Democracy

Political parties serve democratic interests as they pursue their own narrower interests. Democracy, popular control of government, does not happen easily; it requires appropriate institutions and practices. The United States is a single nation that also contains vast differences, as Joseph Romance emphasizes in his essay. Spread across seven time zones from east to west and five thousand miles from north to south, the country varies enormously in topography and climate, from the icy tundra of Alaska to the humid swamplands of Florida. Its diverse political cultures range from traditional New England's commitment to a cohesive commonwealth to southern California's pursuit of individualistic self-fulfillment.[13] Members of virtually every religion and ethnic group in the world live in the United States, a "universal nation." A quarter of the population already is different from the historic European stock, and these groups may become a majority of the total population in the next few decades.[14]

Politics creates unity from this kaleidoscopic diversity. Their common creed, their common institutions, their common political practices enable the citizens of the United States to act both collectively and peacefully, to channel ambition, to determine policies. It is not simple—compare politics in the United States to either the authoritarian regime of another large nation, China, or the fratricidal conflicts of a small country such as Bosnia.

Democratic politics is especially difficult. It may be relatively simple to govern when the principle of rulership is force, when power "grows out of the barrel of a gun," as Mao Tse-tung declared. It is far more complicated when, as premised in the Declaration of Independence, the ruling principle is that governments are legitimate only when "deriving their just powers from the consent of the governed."

Democratic politics means more than majority rule. Elections can choose officials by majority vote, but electoral verdicts are too general to guide these officials. Opinion polls can give us some measure of majority opinion, but they cannot resolve the complexities of public policy. Even if elections were always based on issues and public opinion polls were always representative and accurate, they cannot provide the deliberation, inclusiveness, and specialized expertise needed in any government.

Democracies also have a unique problem. They value popular rule, but cannot assure popular participation. Politics is usually of only limited significance to most persons. Most often, people spend their limited time on their careers or education, their families and relationships, and their sparse leisure hours. Politics is remote, hard to understand, and difficult to influence, while personal effort is more likely to affect our jobs, our love life, our bowling score. Political parties meet this problem; their special function is creating connections between the populace and the government, to give meaning to the "dependence on the people" that Madison described as "the primary control on the government."[15]

Political parties fulfill this function in several ways, while also seeking to promote their own interests in power. Most generally, they organize the electoral process, simplifying the choices presented to a busy citizenry. It is much easier for a voter to choose a Republican or a Democrat (or a Reform Party aspirant) than to seek information about candidates with unknown characteristics. For ambitious politicians, these labels make it easier to win support at the polls.

In organizing elections, parties promote popular participation. They seek those voters who are supportive or may be persuaded. Even today, as in the fabled days of the urban machine,[16] the parties are active in bringing new voters and immigrants to the polls, socializing them to the electoral process. In their contest for power, they draw attention to the elections and work to get out the vote on Election Day. Fostering emotional ties to their own causes, symbols, and leaders, they also foster attachment to American government in general.

In their search for victory, politicians provide information critical to popular rule. Their party labels associate them with a historic record, and with particular policies, so that voters can make their choices without an extensive, and usually unnecessary, search for information.[17] With no additional effort, a voter can assume, for example, that a Democratic candidate probably leans toward right-to-choice on abortion and that the Republican candidate probably favors the right-to-life position.

To win office, parties become attuned to popular demands. Precisely because they do not always "stand on principles," the parties are ready to respond to the voters' wishes. When public opinion seemed to favor Perot's advocacy of a balanced federal budget, for example, President Clinton and the Democratic Party adopted this program. When public opinion turned against the Republicans' shutdown of the federal government in 1995, on the other hand, the party beat a retreat and accepted much of the federal spending it had previously condemned.

Parties serve democracy by promoting the resolution of political differences and developing public policy. Their interest in policy programs comes partly from their own beliefs. Politicians do, in fact, have principles and there are wide differences between Republican and Democratic Party leaders.[18] Beyond their own principles, however, parties have a need to build a record, to satisfy the needs of their constituent groups, to develop appeals to the electorate. Their self-interest makes parties advocate programs, resolve programs, defend their own programs, and criticize their opposition's programs. In so doing, they promote the public interest in responsive government.

The Party Debate

Despite their service to democracy, the two major American parties are not highly regarded today by the voters. The emergence of Perot and the Reform Party is emblematic of voters' general disdain for the present system and their considerable support for a new or third party. These sentiments raise questions, debated in this book by Professors Romance and Lowi, about the viability and desirability of the existing two-party system.

Public attitudes are uncertain. While the electorate largely does identify with the two major parties, the strength of these loyalties is weak; most voters are willing to select candidates from the other party, to split their tickets, and to change ballot choices from one election to the next. It is rare for candidates other than Republicans and Democrats to win office: there is only one Independent in Congress, and only one Independent governor. Even Perot, flamboyant and well-financed as he is, was unable to win a single electoral vote for president in either 1992 or 1996, and his vote was more than halved between the two contests. But this dominance of office does not prove that citizens are necessarily happy with the limited choices available.

Voter loyalties, however, are not the critical factor. In examining the political parties, we must remember to concentrate on the parties as collectivities of ambitious politicians. The electorate comprises the consumers, the market for these politicians, not the parties themselves. Even with uncertain voter loyalties, the two-party system can remain, as it has persisted, so long as it serves the interest of political aspirants.

Institutional factors have strengthened the hold of the two major parties. The presidency focuses attention on this single executive office, won through statewide pluralities and a national majority in the Electoral College. Along with the single-member, plurality system of congressional election, these institutions tend to restrict competition to only two viable candidacies, the others derided as "wasted" votes. Furthermore, the parties reinforce their built-in dominance through election laws, which give them advantages such as automatic placement on the official list of candidates and some public financial subsidies, while discouraging new parties through various barriers, such as requiring complicated petition signatures to win a place on the ballot.[19]

Change toward a three-party system would require that some political leaders see the new system as serving their interests. The Republican Party came to predominance in such circumstances at the time before the Civil War,[20] and it is not impossible that contemporary conditions would induce enough politicians to take a new electoral plunge. If public opinion turns further against the two major parties,[21] if presidential-congressional gridlock fails to resolve major current issues, if an economic or foreign policy disaster occurs, political entrepreneurs may be willing to launch and sustain such a peaceful revolution in American politics.

Would a new system benefit the country? Even if it were possible, even if it meets the needs of politicians, surely this is the predominant question. Would three, rather than two, parties better fulfill their public functions? There is no sure answer, and "reforms" often turn out different, even worse, than expected—as the campaign finance laws demonstrate—but we can speculate.

Participation in elections is likely to increase, as it did in 1992, when the Perot candidacy brought new voters to the polls. On the other hand, elections may be more confusing to these voters. The simple "yes-no" option of the two-party system would now be complicated by "strategic" balloting. Voters would need to decide not only whom they preferred, but whether their vote for one candidate, for example, the Reform nominee, was indirectly helping their least preferred candidate, a Republican or Democrat, to win.

Lowi is probably correct in arguing that a three-party system would bring more issues into the public debate, as each group explored the political terrain for items that would increase its popularity. It is not obvious, however, that these issues would be more easily resolved. Assembling a congressional majority is difficult enough when the negotiations are two-sided. Would there be more compromise and cooperation when there are three contestants? Would a president be more or less able to win support for his agenda when he begins with even fewer members of his own party?

More generally, we may wonder about the effect of a three-party system on the social and political stability of the United States, an issue emphasized by Romance. Each of the parties would be more clearly linked to its constituent base, more "responsible" to them. Freed of the need to seek a majority, however, what would induce these parties to seek the support of other groups, to be "responsible" for meeting general national needs?

There are many means to improve America's political parties, and surely there is much to remedy in the American condition. A three-party system, or even more parties, is one possible direction of change. Other paths are suggested in the documents included in this volume. Perhaps we can still hope, as an earlier scholar did, that "Whatever America finds necessary to do in the years to come, the politics of American democracy will surely make possible."[22]

Notes

1. Clinton Rossiter, *Parties and Politics in America* (Ithaca, N.Y.: Cornell University Press, 1960), 1.

2. Stephen Salmore and Barbara Salmore, *Candidates, Parties, and Campaigns* (Washington, D.C.: Congressional Quarterly, 1985), 243.

3. Kevin Phillips, *Arrogant Capital* (Boston: Little, Brown, 1994), 29.

4. John H. Aldrich, *Why Parties?* (Chicago: University of Chicago Press, 1995), 296.

5. Alexis de Tocqueville, *Democracy in America*, ed. Phillips Bradley [1835] (New York: Vintage Books, 1954), vol. I, 185.

6. M. Ostrogorski, *Democracy and the Organization of Political Parties* [1902] (New York: Anchor Books, 1964), 309, 315.

7. "Whoops, More Evidence to Ignore," *The New York Times* (December 10, 1997), A28.

8. I borrow this section title from Aldrich, who has the best contemporary theory of American parties.

9. *Thoughts on the Causes of the Present Discontents,* in *The Writings and Speeches of Edmund Burke,* ed. Paul Langford (Oxford: Clarendon Press, 1981 [1770]), 317.

10. E. E. Schattschneider, *Party Government* (New York: Holt, Rinehart, and Winston, 1942), 35.

11. John F. Kennedy boosted his presidential ambitions by describing such cases in a book on unusual senators, *Profiles in Courage* (New York: Harper, 1956).

12. Aldrich, 21–24.

13. See Daniel Elazar, *The American Mosaic* (Boulder, Colo.: Westview Press, 1994).

14. See Ben J. Wattenberg, *The First Universal Nation* (New York: Free Press, 1991).

15. James Madison, *The Federalist, No. 51* (New York: Modern Library, 1941 [1788]), 337.

16. See the classic work of William Riordan, *Plunkitt of Tammany Hall* [1905] (New York: E. P. Dutton, 1963).

17. The voter's search for information is a critical element of Anthony Downs' important theory of political parties. See *An Economic Theory of Democracy* (New York: Harper, 1957), part III.

18. The evidence is overwhelming. On the beliefs of party leaders, for example, see the poll of 1996 national convention delegates in *The New York Times* (26 August 1996), A12. On the differences in Congress, see David Rhode, *Parties and Leaders in the Postreform House* (Chicago: University of Chicago Press, 1991).

19. Steven J. Rosenstone, Roy L. Behr, and Edward H. Lazarus, *Third Parties in America,* 2nd ed. (Princeton: Princeton University Press, 1996), chap. 2.

20. Aldrich, chap. 5.

21. See David King, "The Polarization of American Parties and Mistrust of Government," in Joseph S. Nye, Jr., et al., *Why People Don't Trust Government* (Cambridge: Harvard University Press, 1997), chap. 6.

22. Rossiter, 188.

Part One

Debating the Two-Party System

1

Toward a Responsible Three-Party System: Prospects and Obstacles

Theodore J. Lowi

One of the best kept secrets in American politics is that the two-party system has long been brain-dead—kept alive by support systems like state electoral laws that protect the established parties from rivals and by public subsidies and so-called campaign reform. The two-party system would collapse in an instant if the tubes were pulled and the IVs were cut. The current parties will not, and cannot, reform a system that drastically needs overhauling. The extraordinary rise of Ross Perot in the 1992 election and the remarkable outburst of enthusiasm for his ill-defined alternative to the established parties removed all doubt about the viability of a broad-based third party. It now falls to others to make a breakthrough to a responsible three-party system.[1]

At the same time, any suggestion of the possibility of a genuine third party receives the cold shoulder from the press and bored ridicule from academics. This reaction should surprise no one. Like the established parties themselves, social scientists are rarely given to innovation; they are almost always on the side of conventional wisdom, proven methodology, and the prevailing canon of their disciplines. Political scientists may call two-party doctrine a paradigm rather than canon, but they are no less loyal to it. With almost religious zeal, the high priests of the two-party system have preached the established faith, and their students who became leading journalists have perpetuated the two-party dogma. Thus, impetus for reform is about as unlikely to come from professors as from precinct captains.

To be sure, a great deal of scholarly analysis has been advanced to explain why third parties quickly disappear and why the two-party system is both natural and virtuous. Political scientists who believe this hold that the traditional Anglo-Saxon electoral system—based on first-past-the-post, single member districts—produces the two-party system by routinely discouraging

3

new parties. They reason that since there can be only one victor in each district, even voters who strongly favor the candidate of a third or fourth party will ultimately vote for one of the two major candidates to avoid wasting their vote and also to avoid contributing to the victory of the least preferred of the major candidates. (This has been elevated to the status of a physical law, called "Duverger's Law" after its most prominent purveyor.) A two-party system is the best of all possible worlds, they hold, because it produces automatic majorities, enabling the victorious party to govern effectively for its full term of office.

Interestingly enough, although many scholars present the two-party system as being inevitable, it has never been left to accomplish its wonders alone. It has been supplemented by primary laws, nomination laws, campaign-finance laws, and electoral rules that are heavily biased against the formation and maintenance of anything other than the two-party system. And even with all that nourishment, two-party systems have prevailed in only a minority of all electoral districts in the United States since 1896. Most of the districts, from those that elect members of state legislatures up to the state as a whole in presidential elections, have in fact been dominated by one-party systems. During the past century, most of our larger cities and many counties, especially those governed by political machines, were admired by social scientists for their ability to overcome governmental fragmentation and to integrate immigrants into electoral politics even as they preached the gospel of the two-party system. While crusading reformers attacked the machines, most political scientists continued to defend them, even while they criticized specific abuses. Although academics are often aware of the deficiencies and strengths of parties, their commitment to the present system prevents them from considering a new one.

It is now time for a frank, realistic discussion of alternatives. No amount of tinkering, adjustment, reorganization, or aggressive public relations campaigns can bring back to life a party system that on its own devices would surely have crumbled a long time ago and that remains vibrant only in the hearts of party practitioners and political scientists. It is becoming increasingly clear that the usual scapegoats—divided government, campaign practices, scandals—are not the problem. The problem is, and always was, to be found within the two-party system itself.

The Constituent Function of American Parties

Much of the reluctance on the part of scholars to jettison myths surrounding the two-party system stems from a fundamental misconception regarding the true function of American parties. As I have argued elsewhere and at some length,[2] parties perform a *constituent* or *constitutional* role in the American polity. Because this notion bears directly on my argument concerning the need for a responsible three-party system, a brief summary is in order.

By stating that parties perform constituent functions, I am not suggesting simply that they represent certain groups or individuals—all parties at least try to represent some segment of the public. Instead, I am using the term in a much broader sense, meaning "necessary in the formation of the whole; forming; composing; making as an essential part." Constituent means that which constitutes. Constitution is the setting up of the way in which a political regime is organized and the laws that govern its organization. Parties have played a crucial role—intended or not—in "constituting" the American political regime by providing much of the organization and rules by which it is structured, staffed, and operated.

This view of party rests upon the distinction between constituent processes on the one hand and policy processes on the other. Political parties may perform both constituent and policy functions; such parties have been labeled as "responsible." American parties have almost never been responsible, policy-making parties, and most reform efforts to make them so have failed. On the other hand, political parties may perform only constituent functions; such parties have been variously called "pragmatic" or "rational-efficient." American parties have nearly always been constituent based, and attempts to improve their organizational capacity in this regard have often succeeded. Indeed, the genius of the American party system, if genius is the right word, is that it has split the regime from policy, keeping the legitimacy of the government separate from the consequences of governing.

One important effect of constituent parties has been the lack of development of American political institutions, even as the society grew and modernized dramatically. A careful review of American history reveals several important regularities of the two-party system. First, the formation of new parties (or the dissolution or the reorganization of existing ones) produces changes in the nature of the regime, while the functioning of established parties does not. In fact, the shift from new to established parties has been accompanied by a parallel shift in the effects of party, from liberal to conservative, from innovation to consolidation, or from change to resistance to change.

Second, new ideas and issues develop or redevelop parties, but parties, particularly established ones, rarely develop ideas or present new issues on their own. Party organizations are thus vehicles for changes in policy originating in other places, but they are not often incubators of policy alternatives. Once a system of parties is established, the range and scope of policy discussion is set, until and unless some disturbance arises from other quarters. Third, the key feature of the functioning of constituent parties has been the existence of competition and not so much what the competition was about. The more dynamic and intense the level of competition, the more democratic parties become, often in spite of themselves. But the more regularized and diffuse the

competition, the more conservative the parties become. The key to understanding the two-party system, and the current necessity of a genuine third
party, lies in understanding these regularities.

During the first party period, roughly from 1789 to 1840, parties served a
liberating, democratic role. To begin with, the new parties helped democratize
the presidency. The first great organized effort to carry an opposition candidate, Thomas Jefferson, into office in the campaign of 1800 was a giant step
toward the plebiscitary presidency—namely, the pledging of electors. By such
means the election of the president was decentralized and popularized by the
parties. The growth of parties directly checked or reversed tendencies toward
a "fusion of powers" at the national level, mainly through the influence that
the new parties exerted upon recruitment and succession of leaders.

The new parties also helped disperse national power by encouraging the
formation of local organizations. The election of Andrew Jackson, the first
rank "outsider," and the nominating, organizing, and campaigning of professional politicians around Martin Van Buren increased participation in the regime. The existence of vibrant organizations dedicated to the pursuit of many
offices provided the raw material for opposition and debate. Grand alliances
of these organizations made it possible to coordinate the activities of officeholders in a fragmented governmental system. Finally, the new parties helped
democratize the electorate. This effect is easiest to document by the sheer
expansion of political activity at local levels. As a result of the expansion of
organized political activity, individual involvement also spread greatly and
mass participation in nominations and elections became highly visible at all
levels of public office. The spread of political activity helped increase the
size of the electorate and produced increasingly large turnouts. None of these
consequences of the emerging parties were particularly policy oriented, of
course, but the process of party development linked elites to masses around
the key issues of the day.

By the 1840s, however, the national party system seemed to pause in its
development. Parties would henceforth monopolize all important elections
and party machinery would dominate, if not monopolize, all nominations.
Parties would also monopolize the procedures and administration of Congress
as well as virtually all of the state legislatures. The schemes of party organization and procedure were to remain about the same for decades to come. Parties
no longer served a liberating or democratic role, but rather a constricting,
conservative one. With a few exceptions, the two-party system has functioned
this way ever since.

The tendencies of established parties were as nearly opposite to those of
new parties as is possible in a dynamic, modernizing society. For one thing,
the established parties contributed to the status quo in government structure.
For example, they helped maintain the centrality of federalism, even as the
national government and the Constitution expanded to meet the problems of

a nationally integrated country. Political leaders, including members of Congress, developed a fundamental stake in the integrity of the state boundary because it was the largest unit for electoral office. This force has had a powerful impact on the substance of much important national legislation throughout the last century, from social insurance to environmental protection. Parties have participated in a silent conspiracy to prevent policy innovations from departing too far from eighteenth-century constitutional structure.

The established parties also made elective offices less democratic by resisting leadership change and policy innovation. From the courthouse to the White House, the parties have not of their own accord brought new elites to the fore or offered powerful checks on existing elites. Neither do they regularly bring new issues to the fore. It has been rare for the two major parties to take opposite stands on new controversies; it is much more common for new cleavages to develop within the existing parties, providing incentives to avoid addressing these controversies.

Finally, there is little evidence to suggest partisan competition has any real impact on electoral mobilization. In many instances closely balanced parties appear to have actively resisted further democratization of the electorate. Expanding the franchise to new voters and mobilizing existing ones often threatens existing party coalitions, and thus established parties have reasons to ignore or actively oppose such expansions. Along these lines, established parties have an investment in existing social cleavages and no real interest in building a consensus across the myriad of ethnic, religious, and regional groupings that characterize American society.

Of course, there have been a few important instances since the 1840s when the established parties have been programmatic and innovative. At such times—most clearly in 1856–60, 1896–1900, 1912–14, and 1933–35—significant differences appeared between the parties and they became innovative rather than conservative. Each period was ushered in by the "redevelopment" of one of the established parties after an earlier political disaster. Such reorganization made the party oligarchies more susceptible to direction from interest groups with strong policy commitments. Party leaders also became more susceptible to mass opinion, partly as the result of the mobilization of new social movements, but also due to increased competition from rivals. And in these periods, the appearance of a third party was a powerful force in implementing these changes. Of course, these third parties eventually faded, once the major parties stole their message and followers, and reestablished a new, conservative equilibrium.

The Two-Party Impasse

Back when the federal government was smaller and less important, the two-party system could carry out its constituent functions without much regard to ideology or policy. Its unresponsiveness produced major political blunders from time to time, but the system was able to right itself after a brief period of reorganization. But with the New Deal and the rise of the welfare state, the federal government became increasingly vulnerable to ideological battles over policy. Even then, such problems were not particularly noticeable while the government and the economy were expanding, but in the early 1970s class and ideological conflicts began to emerge more starkly, and the two-party system was increasingly unable to offer productive competition.

Thus were born the familiar "wedge" issues—crime, welfare, prayer, economic regulation, social regulation, taxes, deficits, and anticommunism. No matter what position party leaders took on such issues, they were bound to alienate a substantial segment of their constituency. While the Democrats were the first to feel the cut of wedge issues, particularly concerning race, Republicans are now having their own agonies over abortion, crime, foreign policy, and budget deficits. Wedge issues immobilize party leadership, and once parties are immobilized the government is itself immobilized.

Party leaders have responded to this gridlock not with renewed efforts to mobilize the electorate but with the strategy of scandal. An occasional exposure of genuine corruption is a healthy thing for a democracy, but when scandal becomes an alternative to issues, leaving the status quo basically unaltered, it is almost certain that all the lights at the intersection are stuck on red. In fact, the use of scandal as a political strategy has been so effective that politicians have undermined themselves by demonstrating to the American people that the system itself is corrupt.

The established parties have atrophied because both have been in power too long. In theory, a defeated party becomes vulnerable to new interests because it is weaker and therefore more willing to take risks. But for nearly forty years, both parties have in effect been majority parties. Since each party has controlled a branch of government for much of that time, neither is eager to settle major policy issues in the voting booth. Voters find it difficult to assess blame or praise, making accountability judgments and partisan affiliation difficult. A very important aspect of the corruption of leadership is the tacit contract between the two parties to avoid taking important issues to the voters and in general to avoid taking risks.

Even a brief look at the two established parties reveals the urgency of the need for fundamental reform, and any remaining doubt will be removed before the end of the Clinton administration. The established parties do not lack for leadership, and with briefing books a foot thick and plenty of economists-for-rent, they certainly do not lack for programs. Here Ross Perot certainly was right: Washington is full of plans, good plans, that the two parties turn into useless parchment. The Republican and Democratic parties are immobilized by having to promise too many things to too many people.

Republicans say that they consider government to be the problem, not the solution, particularly in economic matters. Yet, to attract enough voters to win elections, they have also pushed measures designed to make moral choices for all citizens; for example, restrictions on abortions are hardly the mark of a party that distrusts government action.

The Democrats like government action: the commitment of government to new programs with grandiose goals and generous budgets is, for them, tantamount to solving problems. President Clinton, for example, took bold stands on a multitude of issues during the campaign, but he conveyed no sense of priority among them. Once in office, Clinton quickly conceded the impossibility of the task he had defined. As the *New York Times* put it in a headline on its front page: "Clinton, after raising hope, tries to lower expectations."

As in the past, the present two-party system functions to keep leadership, succession, and governmental structure separate from the actual settlement of issues. The tendencies of the established parties to preserve institutional structure, avoid issues, and stifle competition are too far advanced for easy reversal. It is time for a new party organization, championing new ideas, to make the party system more competitive, as the original American parties did. A genuine third party would shatter this conservative alliance, jump-start the development process, and once again make parties agents of liberation, democracy, and innovation.

The Impact of a Genuine Third Party

Predictably, defenders of the two-party system have devoted considerable energy to shooting down any suggestion that the status quo can be improved upon. They have produced all sorts of scenarios about how a third party could throw presidential elections into the Congress, with the House of Representatives choosing the president and the Senate choosing the vice president. Worse yet, if it survived to future elections, a third party would hold the balance of power and, as a result, wield an influence far out of proportion to its electoral size. It might, by its example, produce a fourth or a fifth party. And if it elected members to Congress, it might even inconvenience congressional leaders in their allocation of committee assignments. There is a great deal of truth in these scenarios: a genuine third party might well cause such things and as a consequence help reconstitute the American regime.

With three parties, no party needs to seek a majority or pretend that it is a majority. What a liberating effect this would have on party leaders and candidates, to go after constituencies composed of 34 percent rather than 51 percent of the voters. When 51 percent is needed, a party or candidate has to be all things to all people—going after about 80 percent of the voters to get the required 51 percent. A three-party system would be driven more by issues, precisely because parties fighting for pluralities can be clearer in their positions. Third parties have often presented constructive and imaginative programs, which have then been ridiculed by leaders of the two major parties, who point out that third-party candidates can afford to be intelligent and bold since they cannot possibly win. But that is the point. In a three-party system, even the two major parties would have stronger incentives to be more clearly programmatic, since their goal would be more realistic and their constituency base would be simpler. Thus, each party could be a responsible party.

Two factors would help prevent the fragmentation that multiparty systems sometimes cause abroad, as in Israel. First, the American electoral system is not based on pure proportional representation. That system, allowing a party garnering a small number of votes to send at least one representative to the legislature, benefits the smallest of parties. Second, the fact that voters formally elect the chief executive provides incentives for splinter parties to coalesce behind one candidate. In a classic parliamentary system, even a party that has elected only a few representatives can exert a disproportionate influence on the selection of a premier.

Flowing directly from three-party competition, voting would increase, as would other forms of participation. Virtually our entire political experience tells us that more organized party competition produces more participation. And we already know that genuine three-party competition draws people into politics—not merely as voters but as petition gatherers, door knockers, envelope lickers, and $5 contributors—making the three-party system an antidote to the mass politics that virtually everybody complains about nowadays.

Even defenders of the two-party system criticize the candidates' reliance on television, computerized voter lists, mass mailings, and phone banks—which dehumanize politics, discourage participation, replace discourse with ten-second sound bites, and reduce substantive alternatives to subliminal imagery and pictorial allusion. And the inordinate expense of this mass politics has led to a reliance on corporate money, particularly through political action committees, destroying any hope of collective party responsibility.

These practices and their consequences cannot be eliminated by new laws—even if the laws did not violate the First Amendment. A multiparty system would not immediately wipe out capital-intensive mass politics, but it would eliminate many of the pressures and incentives that produce its extremes because third parties tend to rely on labor-intensive politics. Third parties simply do not have access to the kind of financing that capital-intensive politics requires. But more than that, there is an enthusiasm about an emerging party that inspires people to come out from their private lives and to convert their civic activity to political activity.

Finally, the existence of a genuine third party would parliamentarize the presidency. As noted above, once a third party proves that it has staying power, it would increase the probability of presidential elections being settled in the House of Representatives, immediately making Congress the primary constituency of the presidency. Congress would not suddenly "have power over" the presidency. It has such power already, in that the Constitution allows it complete discretion in choosing from among the top three candidates. But if Congress were the constituency of the president, the president would have to engage Congress in constant discourse. The president might under those circumstances have even more power than now, but he would have far less incentive to go over the head of Congress to build a mass following. Even now, with two parties based loosely on mythical majorities, a president cannot depend on his party to provide a consistent congressional majority. The whole idea of an electoral mandate is something a victorious president claims but few members of Congress accept, even for the length of the reputed honeymoon. Thus, current reality already forces the president to bargain with members of the opposition party.

Confronting three parties in Congress, each of whose members were elected on the basis of clear policy positions, the president's opportunities for bargaining for majority support would be more fluid and frequent. In our two-party environment, issues are bargained out within the ranks of each party and often never see the light of day, particularly during the session prior to a presidential election. A third party with a small contingent of members of Congress would insure a more open and substantive atmosphere for bargaining to take place—after the election.

A genuine third party would play the role of honest broker and policy manager because it would hold a balance of power in many important and divisive issues. There would be little fear of the tail wagging the dog because, unlike European parties, Democrats and Republicans are not ideologically very far apart—they have simply not been cooperating with each other. The presence of a third-party delegation gives the president an alternative for bargaining, but if the new party raised its price too high it would simply give the president a greater incentive to bargain with the other major party. Another important myth in the United States is that policy making is a matter of debate between the affirmative and the negative. But simple yea versus nay on clearly defined alternatives is a very late stage in any policy-making process.

Over time, a three-party system would alter the constitution of the American regime. Very quickly and directly, the entire pattern of recruitment and succession would change. The separation of powers would begin to recede until the presidency and both houses of Congress had become a single institution. The function of the cabinet and the very purpose of cabinet officers would change. These patterns would develop whether the lead issues were crime, economic development, health care, or foreign affairs. The parties would inevitably be more policy oriented and responsive to the public will.

The point here is that the third party is a liberating rather than a confining force, a force for open debate on policies. Just as the rise of the two-party system fundamentally altered the constitutional structure of our government appropriately for the nineteenth century, so a three-party system would alter the structure appropriately for the twenty-first century.

Toward a Genuine Third Party

Immediately, one must add an important proviso: A genuine third party must be built from the bottom up. It must be an opportunistic party, oriented toward the winning of elections. It must nominate and campaign for its own candidates at all levels and not simply run someone for president. Of course, building such a party will be difficult. It will require mobilizing a large number of people and resources. And it must attract regular Democrats and Republicans by nominating some of them to run as candidates with the third-party nomination as well as that of their own party. Joint sponsorship has been practiced by the Liberal and Conservative parties in New York for decades. Being listed on two lines on the ballot is a powerful incentive for regular Democrats and Republicans to cooperate with a new party, if not to switch over. About forty states have laws preventing or discouraging this practice, but their provisions will probably not stand up to serious litigation.

Although a genuine third party will not be able to elect a president, it must elect enough legislators to make a difference. This was a big error for Ross Perot when he ran for president. Not only did he mistakenly assume he could win, but even if he had won, he would not have had a majority in Congress; in fact, he would have faced a very hostile Congress. Perot would have been able to carry out none of his programs. Thus, a third party may present voters a clear set of policy alternatives but it must be clear on what it can accomplish. It is not a governing party; it must pursue means other than taking over the government in order to implement programs.

Here history provides some good examples. While genuine third parties have been infrequent in the United States, whenever they have organized from the bottom up they have had significant and generally positive effects on the regime. One of these is providing a halfway house for groups "wedged" out of the two larger parties. In 1924, the progressive movement succeeded in forming the Progressive Party in Wisconsin and other midwestern states, which nominated Robert M. La Follette for president. In the 1930s, the Farmer-Labor Party flourished in Minnesota, where it eventually fused with an invigorated Democratic Party. In the process, both of these third parties provided the channel through which many dissident and alienated groups found their way back into politics, and their influence lingered long after the parties themselves. Similarly, wherever the Dixiecrats organized as a party, that state was later transformed to a genuinely competitive two-party state.

Of course, many third parties in American history have not built from the bottom up, including left- and right-wing splinter factions, protest movements, candidate caucuses, and single-issue interest groups, most of which sought merely to use a presidential campaign to advance their substantive message. Few of these groups have wanted or tried to play a continuing role in the American political system. Here again, Ross Perot provides an instructive example and a warning. After the election, he chose not to institutionalize his campaign by building a genuine third party, but chose instead to found a "citizens lobby," United We Stand America. Our system hardly needs another sophisticated lobby stirring up the grassroots to pressure the established parties, particularly one that is dominated by its celebrity founder. The resources available in the Perot campaign—plentiful money, a dynamic leader, thousands of committed volunteers, and millions of disenchanted citizens—are wasted on such an effort. Just imagine where a third party would be today if a fraction of Perot's expenditures had gone to organizing efforts at the grassroots level to field candidates from municipal elections on up.

There are, however, numerous efforts under way to exploit this opportunity. A national Independence Party was founded in 1992, drawing on many former Perot activists but operating on a party principle rather than a group principle. In 1993, the party's name was changed to the Federation of Independent Parties to accommodate the several affiliated state parties operating under different names. Some predated our national effort, and others were operating in states that do not permit the use of party labels, such as Independent, that have been used before or might tend to misrepresent the size or character of the membership. But as with most such efforts, the national party began to founder in 1994, when at its organizing convention it was split apart by integration with the New Alliance Party. The party changed its name to the Patriot Party and the leaders of the New Alliance Party dropped their name and separate identity in an effort to indicate that they are no longer a fringe party. Although the future of the national party was left very much in doubt, the elements of a real national candidacy were in place. And meanwhile, genuine centrist parties were forming in more than twenty states, some affiliated with the national party and some not. Candidates for governor and Congress and other offices were nominated in 1994, and there was the beginning of real progress toward three-way electoral contests—and also two-way contests where the third party candidate offered at least some opposition to an otherwise uncontested incumbent.

Such efforts that produce few if any electoral victories confirm to mainstream observers the futility of efforts to form a new electoral party. However, if the leaders, organizers, and activists within the new party maintain awareness that victory comes in more than one form—politics is not a game—the chance of persistence and growth is enhanced. So is the ultimate goal of transformation of American politics by turning the two-party system into a three-party system. The results of such a three-party system would be immediate, unlike the long and unintended developments of party reform within the context of the two-party system. The first definite possibility is that the two major parties would, in this three-party context, be able to realize more of their own virtues. The programs and goals of the established two parties are not inherently evil; it is their duopoly that is evil. Both operate as majority parties, both enjoy much of the satisfactions of majority parties and have for a long time. Because of that, they are decadent parties. If power, according to the philosopher, does corrupt, it is usually from having a lot of it for too long a time. The duopoly has to go.

A second consequence, again an immediate consequence flowing from the permanent establishment of a three-party system, is improvement in the legitimacy of political action and public objects. It is no figment of the imagination that the public is receptive to a new third-party organization. The results of the 1992 election reveal that millions of Americans are willing to vote for someone and some party other than the Democratic or Republican. Polls conducted during the most partisan season, the spring and summer of 1992, confirmed that nearly 60 percent of the American people were favorably disposed toward the creation of a new political party.

Meanwhile, personal commitment to the major parties continues to decline and public distrust of politicians continues to increase unabated. The high priests of the two-party system are looking for the explanation everywhere except where the explanation truly resides—in the present party itself. Since the two parties are a duopoly and operate as a duopoly, they have no incentive or will to break open and look publicly at the hundreds of thousands of established coalitions and networks that support the programs that give rise to the deficit and the impossibility of reducing it. There is no way these party leaders can reduce the deficit by screaming at the deficit figure itself and by passing legislation like Gramm-Rudman or constitutional amendments to promise some kind of ceiling on the aggregate figure itself. That is akin to howling at the moon. The gridlock over the deficit and the growing national debt was never attributed to divided government. It was attributed to the two-party duopoly and its primordial stake in the maintenance of the networks of support for existing programs, whether they are still useful or completely outmoded. A third party with no stake in those networks will not immediately bring honesty and integrity to government and will not immediately bring the budget into balance. But it will contribute to honesty in budgeting because it will have every incentive, every selfish incentive, to do so.

Finally, if this new effort to create a genuine third party in a new three-party system accomplishes nothing else, it will at least make a great contribution to political pedagogy and public education. It should be considered a great success if it jolts entrenched political journalism and academic political science toward a reconsideration of their myth-ridden conception of the prerequisite of democracy in general and American democracy in particular. And it can be considered a great success already to the extent that textbooks and classrooms are raising fresh and new curiosities about what really works in a democratic political system. We end as we begin, with the proposition that there is nothing in the universe that demands a two-party system, and therefore it is not sacrilegious to advocate an alternative.

Postscript 1996: The End of the Two-Party System?

The case for a three-party system is stronger today than ever. Popular support for a third party remains well above 50 percent, and even Ross Perot did a 180-degree turn in 1995, choosing to convert United We Stand America from a civic consciousness movement to a political party. This was an important commitment because Perot and associates were fully aware of how tedious, difficult, and expensive it is to gain ballot access for a political party rather than an independent candidate. As of the end of February, Perot's Reform Party had succeeded in gaining ballot access in twelve states, with strong prospects of seven or eight more during the spring.

Sifting the Recent Evidence

Yet, in many important respects, the United States today seems farther away than ever from the end of the two-party system. Here is some of the evidence:

- The 1994 congressional elections produced a spectacular reaffirmation of the party system. Burnham (1996) and others are already recognizing 1994 as the critical realignment election they had been expecting for many years.
- Even without a presidential election at stake, the 1994 election seemed to produce a mandate, in the form of the Contract with America.
- Party discipline has rarely been higher than it was in the first session of the 104th Congress. In fact, we have to reach back toward 1900 to find anything like the party discipline now seen regularly demonstrated in roll call after roll call.
- Divided government prevailed, but it seemed to be virtually an institutionalization of the two-party system, with one party dominating Congress and the other dominating the presidency. This can be seen as a form of party government, with each party being able to behave like a governing party, having control of at least one major branch of the national government.
- With realignment accompanied by institutionalization of the parties in governmental command posts, there was an unprecedented opportunity for "responsible party government" because a mandate plus institutional

power contributed to the clarification, in almost laserlike precision, of the line of accountability between electorate and party.

- Finally, the priesthood within the political science and journalist professions generally embraces with renewed vigor their faith in the virtues of the two-party system as the only way America can be governed. If their faith in the two-party system remained strong despite the weakness of parties and the ambiguities of two-party confrontation, their faith can only be strengthened by the revival, indeed the renaissance, of party discipline and party responsibility.

But these facts do not sustain the brief for the two-party system when they are subjected to cross-examination by means of other facts:

- This is probably the most ideological era of American politics in the twentieth century, and yet the strongest and deepest political controversies are *within* the parties, not between them. Of course, this has been true for a long time, just as Samuel Lubell argued over forty years ago in his still useful book, *The Future of American Politics* (1952: 212): the key to the politics of any period in the United States will be found in the disputes taking place within the majority party.
- This is true now as in Lubell's time because the two-party system is still a duopoly, and like duopolies in the economy, the two competitors tend to move closer and closer toward each other as they discover there is more to be lost than gained from all-out competition. Whatever differences have existed between the Republican and the Democratic parties has practically disappeared during the past decade. They are like McDonald's and Burger King sitting close enough together to be able to share the same exit lane. Bill Clinton is the most recent Republican president, just as Richard Nixon was the last Democratic president.
- The intense and divisive controversies within the Republican Party are rich in policy content as well as ideology, but they are tearing the GOP apart even as they are mobilizing the Republican majority in the House of Representatives and only slightly less so in the Senate.
- The House Republicans led by Newt Gingrich met their Contract obligations and went beyond them. But since most of the items in the Contract and related bills were so consistently within the free market (or "moderate") wing of the Republican Party, every successful roll call contributed to the mobilization and further radicalization of the social issue (or "conservative") wing, inside Congress but also outside Washington at the grassroots.
- This polarization within the Republican Party almost literally destroyed the substantively innovative aspect of the Gingrich revolution. The boldest parts of the House's accomplishments were severely compromised

and weakened in the Senate even before they reached the White House for possible veto. As energetic as the 104th Congress has been, the result has been incrementalism—full of sound and fury, but signifying little.

- As the Republican Revolution went beyond its 100 Days into its 300 Days and 400 Days, its program became less and less popular in the nation, and the popular rating of Congress, already low, declined along with the program. So did the public standing of Newt Gingrich. Few highly visible politicians have ever had the poll negatives to match those of Newt Gingrich.

- Early in the presidential nominating campaign of 1996, the astute David Broder (1996) observed that not only had "none of the Republican contenders [wanted] to embrace Speaker Newt Gingrich," but also that it was striking "that none of the surviving Republican presidential hopefuls is running on the 1994 Contract with America. In fact, the candidate who came closest to embracing the Contract, Senator Phil Gramm of Texas, withdrew after the first two tests, in Iowa and Louisiana."

- Another fundamental contribution to the decadence of the two-party system is the rise of the PACs, having swelled in numbers to more than forty-five hundred. Possibly the most significant contribution they make to politics is to reinforce incrementalism. Whatever impulse to substantive innovation there is in American politics is more than neutralized by the influence of the PACs, which are tied to individual members rather than to a party or to the nation. PACs use their influence to either obtain or protect a specialized law, agency, or decision. This helps explain why not a single major new national government program has been adopted or terminated since 1973—the year the reforms producing the PACs were first adopted.

- Since PACs finance elections, and PACs are found largely outside of the districts where most members are elected, PACs have helped implement a new system of *indirect representation.* Members are elected from geographic districts, but they have a fiduciary obligation to their financial sources outside their districts that at least competes with, if not displaces, their electoral obligations.

- The mischiefs of these particular factions can be appreciated all the more when we add the fact that PACs are a product, a *direct* product of the two-party system. Advertised as a major reform to strengthen political parties and to make them more honest in the wake of the Watergate scandal, PACs were a bipartisan reform. They were the result of an agreement to bring interest groups more directly into the electoral process by legalizing direct corporate financial support of legislative candidates.

All of the items above are not merely developments that have taken place *within* a two-party context; they are developments that have taken place *be-*

cause of the two-party duopoly. Thus, there appears to be nothing new in this most recent strengthening of party lines, except that Republican control of Congress after the 1994 election contributed to the equalization of PAC contributions between the two parties.

Since PACs are protected from abolition by the First Amendment and by the very power that PACs have over members of Congress, the best way to rid ourselves of the PAC scourge is by changing the party system. Moreover, the neutralization or downright obsolescence of the PACs will turn out to be only one of the many advantages to be gained in our democracy from a new multi-party system.

The way to start the process of genuine political reform is to take the present party system off life supports. Political scientists persist in predicting the failure of each and every effort to form a new political party, and the failure of each one is taken as confirmation of their predictions. It is as though "Duverger's Law" not only enjoyed the high status of a physical law but perhaps of natural or divine law because belief in the two-party system takes on the quality of a religion. But the truth of the matter is that third party efforts fail because that is the objective of the electoral laws of every state (where all the relevant electoral laws are made). The legal barriers to a new party and a new party system have proven far too strong for even the most dedicated, broadly based, and best financed new party movements. In response to an assertion made in the neoconservative *National Standard* that "American politics raises no significant technical bar against the existence of third parties," ballot access specialist Richard Winger listed nine formidable legal barriers. Space limitations permit identification here by label only: ballot access, campaign finance, government-funded primaries, timing of nominations, fusion, registration, voter information, representational election boards, and ballot order (*Ballot Access News,* January 14, 1966: 4).

Continued Signs of Change

There are some hopeful signs of change, however, in no small part because of the mobilization of multiculturalism and the legal challenges to make the electoral system more responsive to it. Whatever the challenge, each and every effort to make the present system appear more representative or more accessible only contributes further to the decline of its legitimacy. In other words, there appears to be no way to work out a legitimate and acceptable system of representation while preserving the single-member district system and all of the electoral laws supportive of it. For example, nothing is more likely to destroy the single-member district system than the benign gerrymandering of the districts in order to produce desired outcomes. The history of failed governments and short-lived republics in Europe and elsewhere is filled with clever efforts to redesign the electoral system to reach planned outcomes. This is why each effort at electoral engineering in the United States has been and will continue to be a national embarrassment. Even the Supreme Court has begun to recognize the practical impossibility of electoral engineering. As one electoral law expert put it: "There is nothing you can do in redistricting now that can keep you from getting sued." In its most recent effort, in the October 1995 term, the Supreme Court indicated that "bizarrely shaped" districts designed for prearranged political outcomes will be subjected to "strict scrutiny"—a status reserved for First and Fourteenth Amendment cases.

All such practices are in jeopardy of "strict scrutiny" because these new gerrymandering provisions are so often racial gerrymanders, albeit positive. Another reason is that "like the antifusion laws, they run afoul of the First Amendment." And for the latter reason alone, courts and parties will eventually have to confront the whole question of the constitutionality of the single-member district system. The beginning of the end rests on recognition of the fact that the single-member district system, especially when combined with two parties, will always systematically suppress *any definable minority*. The more identifiable and recognizable the minority, the more hurtful this suppression is to the legitimacy of democracy. Since there is absolutely no way to design single-member geographic districts that will obey the rules of continuity and numerical equality, and at the same time produce satisfactory minority representation, the constitutional support for the single member geographic system will continue to weaken until the courts will have to throw up their hands and give the states no alternative but to abandon districting altogether and go for at-large election of representatives. Statewide at-large election of representatives is not unknown in the United States. There have been a number of instances where states have had to turn temporarily to at-large elections when they were unable to reapportion following a decennial census. At-large election is coming soon, but not soon enough.[3]

The handwriting is already on other legal walls protecting the two-party system. Two lines of litigation are most relevant to the prospects of third party success in the future, but these are not the only constitutional challenges to the system. The first of these is the successful case involving "fusion" in Minnesota. Fusion is the original name for the practice of a minor party nominating another party's nominee, giving that nominee two places on the ballot. Fusion is permitted in only six or seven states. All other forbid it, either by state law or by major parties rules, providing that no candidate can occupy more than one spot on a ballot and can accept the nomination of one party, even if the candidate consents to the minor party's nomination and the other party does not object. Fusion is essential to the growth and durability of only a minor party, as is demonstrated not only by the four-party system in New York State, where fusion is permitted, but also confirmed by the fact that third parties flourished at the turn of the century until barriers to fusion were adopted.[4] In *Twin Cities Area New Party v. McKenna* (January 5, 1996) the

United States Court of Appeals for the Eighth Circuit held that Minnesota's antifusion laws "are unconstitutional because the statutes severely burden the New Party's associational rights. . . ." The Court recognized that it was only invalidating provisions that prevented minor parties from joint nomination where the candidate and the relevant major party consented. It said explicitly that it was not confronting the broader Minnesota statute which states unconditionally that "no individual shall be named on any ballot as the candidate of more than one major political party" because this more general prohibition against fusion without the consent of the major party was not involved in this case.

Litigation in other states producing contrary results makes almost certain that the Supreme Court will in the near future take a leading case on the subject of fusion. In a 1991 Wisconsin case (*Swamp v. Kennedy*), the Seventh Federal Circuit voting three against two, handed down a decision inconsistent with the Minnesota decision. Meanwhile, litigation was under way in at least two other circuits, the Third in Pennsylvania and the Tenth in New Mexico. It is overwhelmingly probable that antifusion laws will not stand up under the strict scrutiny of the Supreme Court.

Another trace of handwriting on the wall against the two-party system is less directly applicable to third-party prospects, but it is still a strong indication of the darkening shadow over electoral laws that protect the two major parties. In late January 1996, the Federal Court of Appeals for the Second Circuit (Brooklyn) agreed with a ruling by a federal district judge that New York's ballot access rules are unconstitutional because they set an "undue burden" on presidential candidates not favored by the party. This meant that the forty-year-old ballot access rules of the state Republican Party, widely considered the most restrictive in the nation, were wiped out. This was another indication of the willingness of federal courts to confront biased electoral laws. In fact, between the ballot access cases and the districting cases, it begins to appear that few if any state protective electoral laws will stand up any longer to constitutional litigation.

[Once the outmoded electoral system goes, so will go the two-party system in most of the states. And so will go the need for minority-oriented reforms, campaign and PAC reforms, and term-limit and electoral college reforms, since the multiparty system that would emerge would put to rest the myth of majority rule, without in any sense endangering the capacity of our legislatures to govern by majority rule. Minorities rule, or plurality rule, was always the American way.] Even in the context of tight party discipline in the 104th Congress, virtually all roll calls on major legislation are the product of coalition building and caucus management. [What is lacking is an appropriate mechanism for representing the minorities and pluralities that make up that electorate. And in a multiparty system, with easier means of forming and reforming parties, economic interest groups (as well as social groups and movements) will find it both necessary and desirable to seek to influence government through the political parties rather than devoting all their political resources to lobbying individual members or capturing relevant agencies.*)*

The specter of a runaway ten- or twenty-party system where a tiny radical party with 2 percent of the representation can dictate policy for the country is the type of bogeyman device that every priest and parent uses to instill faith by fear. Constitutional change will almost certainly produce multimember districts, but these do not have to be statewide in populous states, nor do strict rules of proportional representation have to be adopted, nor will we be forced to convert to a parliamentary system of government. Once the necessity for multimember district representation is confronted, American legislatures will use their natural ingenuity to fashion electoral laws appropriate to our multicultural, plurality-rule country. Whatever system they fashion will be more hospitable to third and fourth parties, without eliminating the first and second parties. Indeed, one of the best features of a "responsible" multiparty system is that it will provide a much healthier environment for the majority parties as well.

Notes

1. This chapter parallels arguments I have made elsewhere, including Lowi 1992a, 1992b, and 1994.

2. See Lowi 1975.

3. In 1995 alone, federal circuit courts were ruling on cases in at least five states arising out of challenges from white plaintiffs who contend that the districts as drawn infringe on their constitutional rights. By the end of 1995, a three-judge federal panel was devising a new map for all of Georgia's eleven congressional districts, following the failure of the Georgia legislature to do the job the previous manner. The Supreme Court threw out the Louisiana "racial gerrymander" case in 1994 on technical grounds, but will surely take it up again as soon as those objections are met by the Louisiana plaintiffs.

4. The Eighth Circuit opinion actually cited the leading article on the practice of fusion throughout the 1800: Peter H. Argersinger, "A Place on the Ballot: Fusion Politics and Antifusion Laws" (1980). This was reprinted as a chapter in Argersinger's book (1992).

1997: Postscript or Obituary?

This conversation actually took place about two weeks before the Reform Party conference in Nashville, January 25, 1997, between the author and Russell Verney, Ross Perot's major domo.

VERNEY: Hello. Professor Lowi, this is Russ Verney calling from Dallas. The Reform Party will be meeting in Nashville in a couple of weeks, and I'd like to ask you your thoughts on what we ought to be discussing and where you think the Reform Party ought to be going.

LOWI: Thanks very much for calling. I've been trying for five years to make direct contact with you guys. I once even got Mr. Perot's fax number from Tom Luce [Perot's former legal advisor], who said it reached virtually into his bedroom. But I got no response from that or from any other of my messages. That's why I took to the op-ed pages, and in the process I learned something I had never realized before, that one turns to the media not because one has influence but because one lacks it.

VERNEY: Well, let's give it a try now. We are concerned about what we are doing in Dallas and how best to relate to the state organizations. As you probably know, we got on the ballot in all the states, and we have some pretty good organizations in a number of states. We hope to pull all that together in Nashville and work toward 2000.

LOWI: I am very pleased about all that. Mr. Perot has made a major contribution to American politics and could continue to do so. I consider it an important victory for the future that Mr. Perot finally became convinced that he should convert United We Stand America from a civic consciousness movement to a genuine political party. We who have been seeking this all along could not get to first base with him for 1996. Tom Luce, in April or May of 1992, in my one substantive conversation with anyone close to Perot, told me flatly that Mr. Perot was absolutely against forming a political party. That's why we went on with our efforts to do it without him, with the formation of the Independence Party, which became, briefly, the Federation of Independent Parties.

VERNEY: You can say he has changed his mind now, and that's what we're up to in Nashville, getting into some new territory, at least for us.

LOWI: Well, you're already too late for a serious presidential run in 2000. That's the trouble with virtually all third parties and independent candidacies. They are inspired to action fifteen months to two years before presidential election, as major parties and their candidates show themselves and begin to heat up the issues and define the points of division. By then, it's already too late—so there is a frenzy of activity, sometimes impressive, as was the case with Perot in 1992 and to a lesser extent, but still impressively, in 1996. At least you are four years in advance this time, but still too late for an effective presidential run. On the other hand, if you organize and focus your party properly now, the 2000 presidential race won't be so important.

VERNEY: Let's take this a step at a time. Being a third party, we have to be concerned with the party's program. We've already had a great impact because of our program, and our future, it seems to me, is tied to what brought us all together in the first place.

LOWI: That's exactly what's wrong, now and before. You should not have been so closely tied to that program in the past, and, whatever value it had in the past, it is not much good to you now, precisely because of your success with it in the past. As is true of virtually all important third-party efforts this century, the influence you've had is on one or both of the two major parties. They've taken over your program, lock, stock, and barrel—deficits and the balanced budget, the national debt and its burden on future generations, and so forth, even the concept of the radical center, which has become Clinton's vital center. That is even more true of the Republican Party. In fact, by the time Tom Golisano ran for governor of New York in 1994, on the Independence Party line (now, I assume, an established Reform Party affiliate), he looked and sounded just like a Pataki clone. It doesn't matter that he had been committed to these causes before Pataki was even heard of as a serious contender for the governorship. By then, however, in the eyes of the New York voters, these issues belonged to Pataki and the Republican Party. I said as much in an op-ed piece in *USA Today* a few days after the 1994 election, with this closing line: "Tom, you might as well have stuffed [your] $10 million in your pipe and smoked it." Golisano has not spoken to me since that time.

VERNEY: But what's the alternative? Party and purpose go together, and what's ours is ours. And without us, the two major parties would not have been such true believers.

LOWI: That doesn't make it right for now. Let's take it step by step, as you asked. The first step has already been taken. You have at last founded a party. The second step has also been taken, at least tentatively: you have formed parties at the state level.

But you've floundered at the third step: you've not been willing to let go; you have not let each state party have the freedom of maneuver to take programmatic stands as they see fit and, especially, to nominate candidates for elective office. I grant that there has to be some central direction if you are to have a national party, but, according to numerous reports from inside the Reform Party ranks (as there had been inside United We Stand America), Dallas is heavy-handed, some say dictatorial. As soon as local chapters (now party organizations) started taking initiatives and acting on their own, a Dallas representative would show up and try to take the situation in hand. Whatever you remember about this, that's the way many of the locals remember it. And that has to stop, in reality and in the impression conveyed. The serious third party must follow the two major parties. It must be real at the state level, real from the bottom up, and as opportunistic as the devil about local worries, local conditions, and locally ambitious people. "In America, all politics is local," said the prophet Tip O'Neill.

VERNEY: I think those complaints were never entirely accurate, but suppose more is left to state parties. What's next?

LOWI: Step four is to change your program. Quit singing the same old song. You can hold to your principles of smaller government, less burdensome taxation, and so forth. But you have to add a new set of ingredients. A Reform Party worthy of the name has to be an *attack party.* Attack what? The two major parties. They, "jointly and severally," are to blame for most of what's wrong in American politics. They are bereft of ideas. Worse, they are a duopoly, and even though they often disagree with each other, they can always agree on one thing (as is true of duopolies in the economy): Suppress competition. This is why there is the equivalent of corporate welfare in the two-party system—because each party depends on wealthy clients and Party A respects the clients of Party B, as a condition of Party B's respect for theirs. This doesn't take collusion or conspiracy. Each knows precisely the needs of the other. And this is where and why there is expanding corruption in campaign finance, and why no substantive campaign finance reform has taken place, despite solemn bipartisan commitments, such as the famous Clinton/Gingrich handshake in New Hampshire in late 1995. By summer 1996, both confessed campaign finance reform was dead for 1996. It's dead, period, as long as we have the two-party duopoly. Thus, the program, the solemn objective, the *Reform* Contract with America is to kill the two-party duopoly.

VERNEY: What do you mean by that?

LOWI: Kill the two-party system. Your aim is not to replace one of those two parties, just as your aim is not to simply get one or both of the parties to accept your program. Note that you already got not only one but both of the parties to accept your program, and so what? Your aim, and therefore your program, should be to add yourself to the system as a third party *in a genuine multiparty system.*

VERNEY: That's not . . .

LOWI: Sorry, that is. You have to break loose in your own mind and in the minds of most Americans from the false God of the two-party system. It was a product of the nineteenth century, and it has been long worshiped by the high priests of political science and political journalism, as well as the party professionals. It is in all the textbooks, and it is a key tenet of the American civic religion. The job of the Reform Party is to expose it for what it has become and to change it by making the Reform Party a genuine party.

VERNEY: The Reform Party campaign can't be a lecture at Cornell. This is the real world.

LOWI: And a very unreal one it is! Just look at what they have done to your program by accepting it! With friends like them, you don't need enemies. That's an unreal world. In the world I propose, you can still attack deficits, but the attack has to be tied to the evils of the two-party system and the blame they deserve for getting us into this mess and keeping us there. And you can attack party finance scandals and even expose and punish some of the perpetrators, but the total absence of effective legislation is in that two-party world that you call real. You don't want to escape a real world for an unreal one, I agree. But why won't you consider escaping the real world of the two-party system with a newly established real world of a genuine three-party system?

VERNEY: What's the difference . . . ?

LOWI: All the difference in the world. First, the whole calculus of victory would be altered. Your presence would move us from a majority orientation—where parties and candidates have to appear to be all things to all people—to a goal of not more than 33 percent of the vote, usually less than that. This is the beginning of the end of deceit—a lovely prospect. Second, you'd have a way to overcome the psychology of the wasted vote. Ever wonder why there is usually such a drastic fall-off from the survey results to the actual vote for even a popular independent candidate like Perot? The people who want to use their vote as a form of protest will stick to a candidate like Perot. But the overwhelming majority of Americans consider politics a game and they want to participate in the game by helping determine the outcome. It is very discouraging to them to have to vote for a candidate they are certain cannot win. They might as well stay out of the game altogether. The effective answer to this is that the voter should consider a third party vote an investment, just like a purchaser of a stock considers it an investment in a new company. This means that a longer view of the vote can be just as rational as a longer view of savings and investment. You wouldn't expect a stock in a new company to pay hearty dividends or substantial capital gain after two or three quarters. Likewise, a vote for a real third party—a party that proves that it is in the system to stay—might still not win this year's election, or the next, or the next; but (1) it could provide the step toward later victories, given the fact that a mere 33 percent plurality could win a seat, and (2) meanwhile, keeping the third party alive gives it a better opportunity to play a balance-of-power between the two bigger parties.

VERNEY: Hmmmm.

LOWI, continuing: . . . but there was a step five we haven't gotten to yet, and that's the biggest step of all: *litigation to change the Constitution.* Here is the real route to the real world of the near future. If there ever is to be a genuine new party, state laws have to be changed. And since there is a party duopoly in every state today—with airtight, albeit implicit, contracts to keep all other parties out—the attack has to be at the constitutional level. A third party in America is like a caste in a caste system—as African Americans were until 1954: Members of a caste can achieve no real participation in their political system by incremental steps. For a caste (and for a third party) the first step has to be through the looking glass, into a new world reality. . . .

VERNEY: (continued silence, with occasional guttural sounds, indicating he was following the line of argument)

LOWI: . . . through the looking glass means that you are facing a situation where you have taken a number of small steps, with the next step, which in a geographical sense is equally small, passing through to another status, another world. The Reform Party in every state should immediately begin to designate nominees for every elective office possible. The only requirements are that they have a respectable work record, can present a decent appearance in public, and can provide at least a portion of their own campaign finance, either out of their own savings or by going into debt. Then, the very minute an election official rejects a nominating petition—for invalid signatures or a broken deadline that is a different deadline from that of the major parties, or any other pretext that can be demonstrated as different from the regulation of the major party candidates—slap 'em with a lawsuit. Plus, wherever possible, select some of your nominees from among the more desirable nominees of the two major parties, and offer them your joint endorsement—that is, create some *fusion* candidates. Forty-three or forty-four states have outlawed fusion since early in this century, and that is the second most important barrier to new parties. (The first and primary barrier is the single-member district system, of which more in a moment.)

One such case, *Timmons v. Twin Cities New Party,* has recently reached the Supreme Court through a victory in the Eighth Federal Circuit (Minneapolis) following an appeal by the State of Minnesota. This was a relatively easy case because the New Party wanted the candidate; the candidate, a Democrat, wanted to accept the fusion nomination; and the Democratic Party officials had given their approval. Yet the law clearly forbids such joint nomination, or fusion, even when all sides agree. The Supreme Court will probably accept it on the same basis laid out by the Circuit Court, arguing that this a blatant case of violation of First Amendment freedom of association. The next case will be much tougher, when a fusion offer is made by the New Party or the Reform Party to a candidate, who already has the major party designation, who wants to accept but the major party refuses to give its consent and is supported by state law.

Present law in all but seven of the states would allow (indeed, might require) the major party to remove their nominee from their own slate if he/she accepts the fusion nomination. There is no way to predict what the court will do in this kind of case, but one thing is certain: If several such suits were brought in different states on constitutional grounds, and if inconsistencies of treatment and reasoning show up from one federal court to another, the Supreme Court would virtually be obliged to review the cases and would find it quite difficult to reject an argument that differential treatment of new parties violates the First Amendment and the equal protection clause of the Fourteenth Amendment. The fact is, anyone who looks at state laws regulating parties, elections, and campaigns would find it very hard to disagree with the argument that very few of the state laws discriminating against new parties would stand up to constitutional scrutiny.

At about this point, Verney had to bid farewell. The only surprise was how long he had stuck with the conversation. What follows is an imaginary ending.

VERNEY: What about the single-member district system? It clearly is the primary protector of the two-party system, but it's been around for a long time and it's backed in federal as well as state law. And it's obviously deeply embedded in American political culture.

LOWI: How right you are. And many people will even believe that it's ordained by the Constitution and perhaps even by providence. That's altogether a myth, but it is a very well established practice. There is absolutely nothing in the Constitution that requires that states take the number of representatives allotted to them by virtue of their population and then subdivide them into congressional districts, with each district electing one member to represent it. And sure enough, after the founding, many states did not bother with districts at all but allowed their members to be elected at large—that is, with each member representing the entire state. The first attempt by Congress to create a uniform national system of representation was made in 1842, with the provision that members of the House of Representatives were to be "elected by districts composed of contiguous territory equal in number to the representatives to which said state may be entitled, no one district may be entitled to more than one representative." Because of widespread disregard of the provision, Congress enacted a much clearer provision in 1872, repeating the districting provisions from before and adding that districts should contain "as nearly as practicable an equal number of inhabitants." In 1901, the requirement of "compact territory" was added, and by 1911 it was as we are familiar with it today: "contiguous and compact territory and containing as nearly as practicable an equal number of inhabitants."

This means that our system of representation in the House of Representatives is not one based on individual voters or on population. It is, in fact, a system of *geographic representation,* and the theory underlying it is that, so long as district lines surround meaningful living units—such as farming communities, or commercial centers, or a homogeneous religious or cultural population, a geographic unit satisfies the requirement of personal representation by enabling the representative to know the real and shared interests of the voters and their families. But, of course, all that changed in the twentieth century, as territories were filled up with masses of highly mobile populations, and as urbanization made these territories far more heterogenous than they had ever been. The distinction between rural and urban was washing out, and suburbia, as well as urban centers, became so dense, as well as so heterogeneous, that every method of drawing district lines was going to be artificial, and every result would create districts that were not homogeneous with regard to any set of interests that could be meaningfully represented. The nineteenth century "Jeffersonian ideal" of stable and homogeneous populations was dead. But the single-member district system of geographic representation went on, and on, and on.

Then one should add the two-party system. This meant that, no matter how the district lines were drawn, the losing party would have no representation at all. Moreover, if the same party regularly lost, consistently lost, it would be composed of a minority, perhaps a minority of 49 percent, that was essentially disenfranchised.

Then add the coming of age of a number of self-conscious minority groups—particularly racial minorities. With or without considerations of party, if such a minority constituted 40 percent of the voting population, but if the person elected was consistently neither a member nor a sympathetic nonmember of that minority group, the minority group was from the start effectively disenfranchised—no matter how legally guaranteed and protected were their votes.

The Voting Rights Act, and federal court interpretations of it after 1965, eventually created a crisis out of these demographic anomalies within the single-member district system. As soon as the courts recognized that there was no way to draw district lines to ensure genuine representation of minority populations by minority members of the legislature, they began to force a breaking away from the legal provision that districts be compact, contiguous, and as close as possible to equal in size. The result: benign gerrymandering. And the outcome is a number of districts that are so ridiculously artificial and stupidly peculiar in size and shape that they must have been designed by people who were dedicated enemies of affirmative action and any other legal approach to racial and other forms of discrimination.

The point here is that there is no way on earth, despite all the goodwill and all the supercomputers, to provide a just system of single-member district representation in a multiracial, multicultural, and multi-interest society. The only way we can reach these goals is to abandon congressional districts and congressional redistricting and all other forms of electoral engineering and go for multiple-member districts with some form of proportional representation. The ideal would be to go back to at-large elections that were widespread before 1842. We would not have to resort to any highly formalized system of proportional representation such as the famous nineteenth-century Hare system that was admired by the illustrious John Stuart Mill. Any form of multiple-member system that gives voters the number of votes equal to the number of members to be elected would solve the problem of multiracial, multiethnic, and multi-interest representation and, at the same time, would remove barriers to important new political parties.

VERNEY: Hold on. You're moving too fast, and you're moving too far. I am amazed that I understand virtually everything you are saying, but you frighten me, because what you envision could produce a five- or ten-party system, and we would have chaos, like France and Italy, or a situation like Israel where you have so many parties that a tiny radical party with only two or three seats in the legislature can exercise enormous power with a threat of depriving the coalition government of a majority.

LOWI: That's a chimera. That's the sort of horrible example that the high priests of the single-member district system and the two-party system will wave in the air to frighten the frail. As long as we have popularly elected chief executives, at local, state, and national levels, and as long as the two major parties continue to exist, there will always be a strong centripetal force toward the fewer, rather than toward the many, political parties. Note, for example, how quickly France moved to a manageable and very effective party system after the Fifth Republic Constitution provided for a strong, nationally elected president along with their premier and their parliamentary system.

VERNEY: That sounds a little bit better, a little bit more reassuring. But where does that leave us?

LOWI: That leaves you in the revolutionary position. This takes us back to litigation. If you build a treasury that permits you to hire a couple hundred litigation-oriented lawyers well trained in electoral law and imbued with the spirit of constitutional consistency, the revolution is in your hands. If Ross Perot had set aside $10 million of the reputed $60 million he spent during the 1992 election campaign just for litigation, he could have started the revolution long ago. First, a few constitutional victories like the *Timmons v. Twin Cities New Party* Minnesota case. After that, the world—that is, the whole world of elections, representation, and political parties.

VERNEY: Is that the only way you feel we'll ever succeed with a Reform Party?

LOWI: That's exactly what I mean. I've thought about this situation from every angle, and I feel I have shared all the disappointments that third-party founders have felt for the past century; and I am convinced this is the time for a new experiment. Everything about democracy is experimental, including all the practice we now follow, whether we question those practices or whether we worship them. It's all an experiment. And after over two hundred years, we are still not able to say that the experiment has passed the test. The best we can say is that the case for democracy is "not proven." We can also say that if we have been experimenting all along, it's time to put the two-party system and the single-member district system that supports it back in the lab and under the microscope. My bet is that if my colleagues in political science and journalism agreed to a discussion of the two-party system in a genuinely experimental spirit, the verdict would be that the two-party system will (1) be found wanting and (2) that it would die a natural death if we pulled out all the legal life supports.

These problems suggest that the great likelihood of a breakthrough for a genuine multiparty system will come from the Christian Right, led by the Christian Coalition. Given the impressive organizational presence of the Christian Coalition in many states, all it has to do is to decide to follow the Perot example and convert their consciousness movement into a political party. Perhaps an interview with Ralph Reed is the next step.

Gridlock and Reform at the Close of the Twentieth Century

Joseph Romance

> First, this great and glorious country was built up by political parties; second, parties can't hold together if their workers don't get the offices when they win; third, if parties go to pieces, the government they built up must go to pieces, too; fourth, then there'll be hell to pay.
>
> *George Washington Plunkitt*

The American political system was designed to be conflict-ridden and it is only because of the emergence of the two parties, and two parties only, that this conflict can be managed effectively without undue harm. The two parties provide a balance between the desire for extensive participation and the need for meaningful and intelligent participation. Furthermore, the two-party system creates the means by which the separate branches of our government can effectively govern. This truism bothers people because it flies in the face of so much of what we want to believe. Americans want more parties because that appears to be more democratic. If only we had more parties, critics assert, we would have better representation, more participation, and a less confusing and more accessible political order. This belief, however, fails to appreciate the constitutional order created by the Founders and ignores the very real and useful functions that the two parties maintain in this most complex of nations.

American politics can be most confusing, not least of all to Americans. Part of that confusion is the direct result of the diversity of American political and cultural life. A nation composed of many immigrants is bound to present a crowded political stage, and citizens are apt to have vastly different perspectives and wants. If the sheer diversity of groups is not enough, our political landscape is cluttered by numerous institutions with a myriad of conflicting responsibilities. This nation is blessed, or cursed, with an elaborate system of administration that includes three separate but powerful branches of government. To complicate the institutional picture even further, this nation is a federal one with fifty powerful and independent state governments—each jealously protecting its own political prerogatives. All these different institutions and groups vie for power in the ongoing experiment that is American democracy. And herein lies the problem. While the states warily preserve their power from possible encroachments by Washington, the nation's capital witnesses an endless competition for ascendancy, as the president jostles with Congress in setting policy and controlling the direction of the nation.

This constant state of strife and confusion about who is in control makes American politics both interesting and frustrating. To many, this discord is actually something of a strength. We live in a system of multiple competing interests in which no one group or institution is fully in control, and thus we are free from political oppression. The pluralist dream of politics is not without its champions, and they often hold up the United States as the greatest example. Pluralists commend the constant conflict between different political groups and believe our system of government, with its checks and balances and frequent elections, allows a fair dispersal of power.

Yet critics of our politics see quite a different picture. In 1995 the nation observed the spectacle of a government shutdown as tourists were turned away from national parks and museums in Washington were closed. While this was certainly no great crisis on the order of war or natural disaster, it lends credence to a recurring complaint about our politics—that this system is so complex and so divisive that fundamental reform is essential. According to one set of critics, such reform is necessary because our leaders are inept or irresponsible and too closely tied to short-term popular opinion. However, a different and more forceful set of reformers fear that our political system is not representative enough and is too elitist and unresponsive. The claims of pluralism are blighted by the inability of the system to represent the poor, the radical middle, or the just-plain-radical, to give a few examples. American politics, instead, is beholden to the status quo and that status quo is protected by the two-party system.

Such calls for reform are a constant theme of American politics and one could chart a history of the nation's politics centered around this demand for change. As one perceptive observer of American politics argues, government gridlock results in the accumulation of problems over time. This buildup of political pressure eventually culminates in the call for extra-institutional reforms to return power to the people.[1] This is apparently a chronic American problem that affects nearly every generation—the source of the problem may vary, but the call for reform is invariable. At the turn of the century, progressive critics of American politics worked hard to curtail the power of the old party machines and found the solution to all our problems in more democratic control over the party organization. The same type of skepticism about traditional political institutions reverberated throughout the 1960s and was a driving force in the various efforts at reform that marked that decade. In response to these criticisms, the political parties significantly altered their presidential nominating procedures by 1972.

The political landscape of the 1990s once again echoes with the sound of anger and animates party reformers' criticisms of governmental gridlock and failures of the political world to fairly represent the citizenry.[2] For many years, political events were a catalogue of Democrats in the Congress battling a Republican president to a virtual standstill as the economy grew worse. The dates have changed and the economy has improved, but recent years offer a simple reversal of political players—a newly Republican Congress challenges a Democratic president over issues of budgets, abortion rights, and political appointees. Time moves on and the parties trade positions of power, but a constant stream of invective issues forth. The debate about gridlock is merely replaced by concerns about dishonesty, which compromises the ability of citizens to control their government. Many of the recent complaints center around the fear of corrupt party financing.

One can hardly blame the public for trying to find fault and it does: The political parties are to blame. Gridlock, corruption, and the inability to think anew about politics is caused by partisanship in our elected officials. As Theodore Lowi, in his essay, bluntly puts it: "It is becoming increasingly clear that the usual scapegoats—divided government, campaign practices, scandals— are not the problem. The problem is, and always was, to be found within the two-party system itself." This diagnosis is often confirmed by the politicians themselves as they rush forth to promise an end to stalemate through a renewed sense of bipartisanship. Thus, one should not be surprised to hear such a consummate party politician as Bob Dole urge the removal of issues like the long-term entitlement problem from partisan debate, arguing that such important matters should not be the political "football" that party leaders use in their games. While some see the solution in getting beyond parties altogether, others, such as Ross Perot and Theodore Lowi, see the solution in more choices. The ideal of choice, so sacrosanct to Americans, provides moral support as critics push for the creation of a third party and insist on reforms that will make such a party a healthy alternative.

But is that true, or even desirable? Blaming the present parties is such a perennial criticism that we are apt to simply accept the reproach without any thought. However, no criticism should be accepted without serious consideration. Before we start changing laws and spending time and money reforming the system, we should be reasonably sure of what we are doing. Let me be clear, a multiparty system would mean significant changes in our political practices and, possibly, would necessitate major reforms to the foundation of our political order. It would require us to rethink federalism, the role of the president, and the very idea of representation as we have practiced it since the founding of the Republic. Political reform should only occur after serious reflection about how our system works and what intentions underlie our different institutions. Political harm results when people fail to realize the wide-ranging consequences of their actions. The political world is such a complicated place that changes are bound to produce other transformations that were not foreseen at first. As we think about the party system and reforms, we should not only ponder the failings of the parties, but we should also consider its successes and how they fit into a wider political and cultural world.

This essay will broadly address the following question: Is the two-party system of Democrats and Republicans to blame for many of the political faults we have today, and is the solution to our problems to be found in encouraging more political parties? The answer is no. If we thoughtfully analyze the nature of our government and consider how parties handle complicated state interests and integrate varied social groups, we come to the conclusion that the two political parties do an excellent job of making American democracy work. One need only look at the actions taken by Franklin Roosevelt to combat the Great Depression to realize that the two-party system does not automatically lead to government inaction and, in fact, the branches of government can move quite quickly to enact significant new programs when guided by the parties. The cause of gridlock and unresponsive government is not primarily found in the two-party system; rather, these problems are a result of the diversity of our nation and the structure of, and the relationship between, our national and state governments. Furthermore, it is not exactly clear that gridlock between the branches of government is necessarily a bad thing. While we might like a government more immediately responsive to our desires, our present government and political parties do a good job of responding thoughtfully to a very diverse nation—culturally, ethnically, and geographically—and more political parties might do a much worse job of making sound public policy out of the cacophony of voices that make up American politics.

The examples of multiparty systems elsewhere are not at all comforting. Israel and Italy, to name just two of the more interesting examples, show us that multiparty systems can be paralyzed by gridlock equal to, if not worse than, the United States. Furthermore, multiparty systems require coalitional governments, which confuse accountability and often force post-election party negotiations to form those coalitional governments. This muddies the connection between the voter and the government team and, thus, it makes participation less consequential. The desire for a responsive government puts much pressure on a plural system and the two parties do an excellent job in balancing the contradictory needs of our democracy. In the end, I will show why the parties enable leaders to work together and make those leaders accountable to citizens, thus making mass, democratic participation meaningful.

I

I will start with a deceptively complex question: Should we have the two parties we have today? In reflecting upon this question, we shall see that political parties represent one of the most perplexing aspects of American political life. They are frequently reviled for corruption and ineffectiveness; and they are not mentioned in the Constitution, so they lack even the intermittent veneration granted the president, Congress, and the courts in American history. From the august pronouncements of George Washington, who urged his fellow citizens to avoid creating political parties, to the most recent generation of college students, who profess independence from the actual parties with an earnestness lacking in any other political statement they might make, Americans view the two political parties with a skepticism bordering on hostile suspicion.[3] If many American political institutions are under fire as this century draws to a close, political parties suffer from the most withering barrage of criticism.

What makes this so puzzling is that political parties are central actors in the story of American politics. Of course, stories need villains and parties are sometimes cast as the evil characters in the tale. However, according to many political scientists and historians, parties are not the villains. In fact, they represent one of the most sympathetic players in the American drama. Political parties, and the two-party system in particular, are an integral force in the rise of democracy. And democracy is the one thing that everyone—average citizens, politicians, pundits, and scholars—agrees is a definite good.

The connection between democracy and parties is best observed by engaging in an exercise in comparative politics. New political parties are springing up all over the world as old, repressive regimes are replaced by new, dynamic experiments in popular government. In Eastern Europe the failed one-party, communist states have been replaced with new, competitive multiparty systems. And, furthermore, it is this very aspect of the regime—the political party—that is frequently mentioned and discussed by citizens of Eastern Europe. Comparatively and historically, there is a direct correlation between democracy and competitive political parties. While many commentators assert American exceptionalism on all sorts of matters, it does not seem that America is exempt from the connections that exist between a well-ordered democracy and the role of political parties.

Of course, these examples might indicate a support for a multiparty system, and most of the countries in the world experimenting with democracy have many parties. However, American political history is a story of the triumph of greater and greater democratic participation by citizens, and this story is accompanied by a robust *two-party system*. What is it about America that makes it exceptional in needing and fostering only two parties? And, in fact, critics of our parties, such as Theodore Lowi, argue that this American exceptionalism—two dominant parties—is the cause of many of our discontents.

The advocates of multiparties suggest that Americans are simply tired of the two parties we have, and of the two-party system itself. This criticism is usually accompanied by the observation that the two parties we have are actually quite similar. Why just these two parties? America is, after all, the land of endless choices. In a nation that offers an array of consumer goods—dozens of different toothpastes, hundreds of television channels to watch, and literally thousands of different kinds of cars—why should we have only two parties to choose from? It seems only fair and American to have more than merely the Democrats and the Republicans as viable choices.[4] However, if a variety of choices is good in principle, why should we limit ourselves to three parties? We could have any number of parties: libertarians, socialists, feminists, African-Americanists, monarchists, and vegetarians could all have their own political parties.

This is not simply a theoretical observation, to be tested in the classroom or debated at wee hours on the Internet. In 1992 Ross Perot launched his bid for the presidency with the backing of no party, just his good intentions and vast wealth, and made one of the best showings ever by an Independent candidate. Some note that he was unique in ways that the news media failed to appreciate. The great challengers to the two-party system in the past had previously been closely associated with one of the two parties, and they often worked to create a party to help them in their effort to win office. In 1912, for example, Theodore Roosevelt was a former Republican president and founder of the new Bull-Moose Party of progressives. He was nominated by a convention and ran with a slate of candidates in many states. Although Roosevelt failed to win, he achieved a second-place finish in that election, besting the Republican nominee, President Taft. In contrast to Roosevelt's efforts, Ross Perot in 1992 did not run as a third-party candidate; rather, he ran as an Independent. He ran alone without a slate of candidates or nomination by a party organization gathered in a convention.

Possibly learning from his experience, Perot emerged again four years later transformed into a party man. Yet he rejected both of the major parties; rather, he made, and continues to make, a serious effort to build a viable third party—the Reform Party.[5] Perot did not run with a team of fellow candidates; however, the Reform Party held a convention and Perot's leadership was challenged by former governor Richard Lamm, of Colorado. Furthermore, today's Reform Party leaders talk about the party after Perot and about running candidates for other offices.

With a little bit of imagination we can see that each of the past three elections (1992, the 1994 mid-term congressional elections, and 1996) revealed a certain possible future for American politics. We witnessed in 1992 a powerful challenge to the party system itself, with Perot's first bid for national office. While the two parties ultimately dominated the final results, nearly 20 percent of the electorate chose to vote for a man with no clear party affiliation. The possibility that Perot, or someone like him, could capture the White House no longer seemed like the foolish musing of political cranks.

Just two years later, however, the congressional elections of 1994 seemed to testify to the well-ordered functioning of the two-party system. Clinton and the Democrats were given a chance to rule in 1992, and enough people were frustrated by their rule to throw the Democrats out and replace them with the established opposition, at least in Congress. One could easily see the "Contract with America" as a genuine representation of an alternative set of policies offered to the nation for their considered judgment. The sheer spectacle of the Republicans taking over the House, for the first time since 1955, was exhilarating to defenders of the established system. (The Republicans, during the Reagan administration, took control of only the Senate.) For those defenders of the two-party system, 1994 was a return to an older partisan politics—the peaceful transfer of power (if only congressional power) from one of the great old parties to another. Finally, 1996 offered us a third possible future with a true third party challenging the two major parties from without and laying the foundation for a long-term existence. While there are many questions about Perot's Reform Party—not the least, its continued dependence on Perot, which makes it susceptible to the charge of being a personal following rather than a party—it is still true that the Reform Party persists and seriously affected the results of the most recent election. If Perot and his followers last, America could see a continual challenge to the major parties for some years to come.

What are we to make of all of this? The past few years reveal a dizzying array of both strengths and weaknesses of the established political parties and the order they helped to create. As they did at the close of the nineteenth century, Americans are questioning their role in the world, worrying about the economic direction of the nation, and searching longingly for the best political arrangements possible in a land so diverse and democratic. To help answer the last query means that we need to think again about what political parties do in our political cosmos. Once again the spotlight is thrown upon the parties, and they must justify their existence in front of a skeptical audience. Despite the example of Ross Perot and his followers and the suggestions of thoughtful critics such as Theodore Lowi, there are very good reasons for America to have only two political parties. These reasons can be grouped into two broad categories: First, there are structural reasons why our political system encourages the existence of only two parties. Yet this is only part of the story. There is also a second category of important reasons that tell us we should be thankful that there are only two parties, even if our political structures were different and allowed for many parties.

The unique arrangements of the American system of government have cultivated the rise of the two-party system. Foremost, the two-party system is fostered by the nature of our political system. Part of this is historical. The two parties, with fair accuracy, reflect the fundamental debate in American politics over the issues of freedom and equality. With a few exceptions, it is usually the Republican Party that fears centralized state action and champions individual freedom. At the same time, the Democrats believe in the government's ability to encourage equality. These principles are central to American politics and the addition of a third party could generate profound philosophical confusion among voters. Furthermore, the two parties are essential in making our government of checks and balances operate, with some degree of efficiency. The ability to create a kind of institutional bridge between the president and Congress, and within Congress itself, makes the two-party system feasible. Finally, the two parties provide a coherent organization to the electoral process. The way we conduct elections and the existence of the electoral college all encourage the development of a two-party system.

Not only have a specific set of circumstances virtually guaranteed that the two-party system would thrive in America, but we should be thankful that this is the case. The two parties make accountability easier in this large and diverse nation. It is much easier to assign blame and to vote the "bums" out if only two parties exist. The addition of more parties would make the control of government more confusing and, thus, the electoral decisions of voters would be more difficult. Participation is vital to democracy, and good participation requires that citizens have meaningful and understandable choices. Because America has so many different ethnicities, religions, and political beliefs, which are both a source of national strength and a tremendous challenge to our nation's leadership, democratic government is profoundly difficult. Few other countries have attempted to mix so many disparate kinds of people together, much less to govern them democratically. Most democracies are found in more homogenous countries. One of the reasons we have successfully integrated such a wide range of peoples is that the two-party system required such peoples and their leaders to work together. Thus, similarities, not differences, are the focus as people find common ground in the two parties. Furthermore, by working together within the party, they cement a political identity— membership in the party itself. While such a bond is subject to constant evaluation and evolution, it transforms the way leaders act and treat each other. Such bonds also exist, to a lesser degree, among voters. The two-party system encourages broad coalitions based on the acceptance of general principles. The acceptance of such common values can only exist after many compromises and with a great deal of tolerance for other viewpoints. What is essential is that these permanent parties, built around diverse coalitions, develop civic loyalty—based on both general values and the political memories that transform narrower allegiances. Although this process has never been easy, it is still one of the hallmarks of the nation.

There is one final reason to be grateful that we only have two parties. A three-party system (or a system of even more parties) would require extensive changes in our political laws and, possibly, amendments to our Constitution, all with the potential for unintended consequences. There is a lot to be said for caution in such fundamental transformations of our system. The two parties represent some of our oldest institutions. We are apt to forget that, although

America is a youthful country, our political institutions, and the Constitution that created them, are some of the oldest in the world. Things that stand the test of time deserve respect, something Americans are not known to easily grant. I think it is something we should attempt more frequently.

Despite the many travails of our history, the stable, powerful democracy our founders envisioned is still with us today. This is a tribute to them and to all American citizens, but, most importantly, it is a recognition of the central role that the two parties have played in the creation and maintenance of democracy.

II

At the simplest level, most political issues suggest a two-party system. After all, when we first think about any controversy, there will always be those in favor of a certain policy and others who are opposed to such policies. Obviously, actual policy issues are more complicated than simply pros and cons, and political problems can suggest numerous solutions; yet the nature of political strife often requires that many conflicts reduce their participants to those in favor of some idea and those opposed to such views. This is often simplified to mean those in control of government and the loyal opposition to that governing team. The problem is that as we consider more issues—as our system becomes more complex—people will have multiple allegiances, which would suggest many parties or a continually shifting set of political alliances. This is the logic behind those who favor more parties: the incredible diversity of issues, which corresponds to the diversity of views held by Americans, demands numerous parties to make the system fairly representative.

However, this will not be the case, because there is an overriding, philosophic dualism in American politics. If it were the case, then two parties would more fully represent the essential foundations of American political debate. In fact, if there was such a dualism, a multiparty system would actually distract us from this central political argument. I believe there is such an overriding dualism that animates political history.

What is this dualism? American history is an ongoing debate about the allure of democracy and the belief in personal liberty. This is not to suggest that political activists in either party march in lockstep to some set of party principles. After all, the pressure to win elections is a powerful way to explain the actions of politicians. As that sage of Tammany Hall, George Washington Plunkitt, once said, "What's the Constitution among friends?"[6] Nonetheless, despite this eloquent plea to move beyond grand principles, many political commentaries, from the classic accounting of American politics offered by Alexis de Tocqueville to more recent works by A. James Reichley, argue that American political history can be reduced to a fundamental divide between those who support popular power and social equality and those who distrust such populism and who are apt to favor individual liberty over the demand for equality.[7] Although many Americans believe in both of these concepts, such ideals necessarily come into conflict at certain points. Moreover, this debate is furthered by the continued political battles between the Democrats and the Republicans. The Republican Party is the party that believes in individual freedom and civil order. In contrast, the Democratic Party, while certainly believing in these ideals, more frequently champions the ideal of social equality. However, we need to explore these two ideals to see how and why they can so easily create disharmony.

This conflict is not obvious to many Americans because we tend to conflate the ideals of personal liberty and social democracy, and they are often synonymous in people's minds. Obviously, these ideals do complement each other. A degree of liberty is essential for a democracy to function, as we need the freedom to speak, to assemble, and to vote effectively. Democracy also cultivates a respect for others and this encourages a wide range of expression that is the hallmark of liberty. However, we should realize that there is an inevitable tension between these two concepts. This does not mean they are always in discord—it means that there is a constant threat that too much democracy will destroy liberty or that extreme liberty will weaken democratic practice. Each ideal continually modifies the other.

First, we must look at democracy. Democracy is the rule of the people. In practice, this means that the majority should decide matters. But what do we mean by "decide matters?" Do most Americans decide what kind of healthcare policy the federal government pursues? Do we hold a national referendum on how much money should be spent on the Defense Department? In America, the majority does not rule directly on matters of public policy. There are a number of reasons for this. In large measure we should note that the nation is too vast for people to meet in a town hall and set policy. After all, a town and a nation are two very different things. The very thing that makes local democracy so appealing is that it implies a politics that rests on personal relationships of familiarity and intimate connections that are impossible at the national level. Still, with recent technological innovations, Ross Perot's vision of a directly democratic "national town hall" becomes feasible, at least as far as voting is concerned. We could have people vote on policies—a national referendum—on many issues, and using television and computers, most of us would not even have to leave home. (One could easily imagine: "Tonight, following *ER*, 'The Democracy Show!' ") As we shall see, though, the American Founders were leery of such direct rule, even if it were possible. Instead, democracy in the United States means that the majority selects leaders who set policy.

Governing is a difficult thing. Policies are complicated, and the need to be fair and effective means that politics should not be left to those who cannot be thoughtful. Government policy cannot simply be the result of mass opinion; rather, it should ideally be the result of considered judgment by the mass of people. The Founders feared, and I believe, that too often citizens act without reason or with too much passion. This is why democracy, while certainly a good thing, is to be embraced cautiously. Good political judgment is the result of reflection on the part of citizens and active guidance of the political agenda by leaders. At least, this is the theory behind representative democracy.

The people, when they act politically, can do things simply because the majority feel that is what should be done. But does this make it right? Suppose the majority decide to imprison the minority? Or, less dramatically, it is possible that the majority might decide to confiscate the property of a certain group. The most basic definition of democracy makes this acceptable. If we held a vote and it was conducted fairly, the decision could be termed democratic. Thus, many critics refer to the dangerous tyrannical impulse that democracies can exhibit. Alexis de Tocqueville persuasively wrote:

> At the present time the most absolute monarchs in Europe cannot prevent certain opinions hostile to their authority from circulating in secret through their dominions and even in their courts. It is not so in America; as long as the majority is still undecided, discussion is carried on; but as soon as its decision is irrevocably pronounced, everyone is silent, and the friends as well as the opponents of the measure unite in assenting to its propriety [8]

While some argue that Tocqueville exaggerates the problem, his observations about a tyranny of the majority are worth pondering and should give us pause when we praise democracy. There is always a nagging question about whether the majority is acting justly. And the first reaction many citizens would have when confronted with an unjust act sanctioned by the majority would be to yell: "What about my rights?" The United States Constitution guarantees the *rights* of individuals to make sure the majority does what is *right*. Which leads us to consider the other aim that the United States Constitution is supposed to foster—the ideal of liberty.

Americans also believe strongly in the principle of liberty or freedom. We are, according to the song, the "land of the free." However, as we have seen, freedom does not necessarily result from democracy. There is a continual threat of democracy thwarting one's freedom. The United States may be a democracy, but it is also a place of great personal freedom. We don't like to be told what to do or how to live our lives. This is also why citizens want more choices; people want the freedom to choose and a multiparty system would apparently provide them with a great deal of political choice.

The two political parties accurately represent the fundamental divide that animates American politics. The *emphasis* that each party places on the principles of equality and freedom helps to clarify American political discussions.

Our love of democracy and equality is most forcefully advocated by the Democratic Party. With matching vigor, the Republican Party maintains a healthy skepticism about equality and the role of government in fostering such equality. In their view, individual freedom is the more central American ideal. From issues such as affirmative action and government regulation of industry, to tax policy, the two parties can be distinguished by their respective stances, grounded in a clear philosophy of politics. This is not to say that every politician acts all the time on these principles or that either party is hostile to the other party's main principles. Instead, I want to highlight a clear and compelling emphasis that each party exhibits.

The Founders recognized the dualism of equality and liberty that is central to American politics. They were fearful of the excesses of democracy and wanted to guarantee the protection of minority rights, but they championed the idea of a popular government that was responsive to the wishes of a thoughtful citizenry. (We should recall, of course, that they had numerous blind spots in their treatment of women and slaves. The definition of citizenship was subject to a long and continual debate.) However, to balance these two forces, they did not envision two parties articulating grand principles; rather, they assumed this debate would occur without parties and that the system of government should try to balance the pressure for more freedom and more democracy. In practice, though, American history reveals the value of each ideal being championed by a distinct party. Such parties can forcefully articulate each ideal, and candidates take their messages to the people under the banners that parties provide.

Complicating this tension between freedom and democracy is the sheer diversity and physical size of the nation. This was true in the 1780s and it is even more true today. Can a diverse nation possibly overcome the problems that the demands of democracy and freedom make? This challenge is daunting enough when one thinks about a homogenous country with people of similar religious and ethnic backgrounds. But the task becomes even more intimidating when more religions, races, and cultures are added to the mix. Yet this apparent problem of so much diversity is transformed into a political asset when the correct government is instituted. The goal was to create a new set of political institutions to moderate all the passions of American political life. The solution, as the authors of the Constitution saw it, is found in the correct structure of government. Our system of government would not need good citizens or benevolent leaders. Instead, we simply need to find the right political arrangements and the competing ideals of democracy and freedom could be balanced and a stable, enduring regime would result. If such a structure was created, the natural ambitions of political representatives would work for the greater good. Individual politicians would be too busy competing with each other to engage in the creation of an oppressive government.

However unexpectedly, this very structure was responsible for fostering a two-party system. We must now look at how and why the Founders built a system of checks and balances and why it helped create, contrary to their hopes, a party system. This turn of events—the development of political parties—struck the Founders as odd and disturbing. They thought that the system they created would not need or favor a party system. Yet, we shall see that by creating a government of separated powers and developing a system of popular control via elections, the two-party system was constructed and nurtured.

III

To many, the problem with our government is that it is inefficient, and this is fostered, even caused, by the two-party system. This is not true. In reality, gridlock results from a fundamental and intentional function of our system of government—the very institutions articulated in the Constitution. Each of the branches of government reflect, in part, the will of the citizens who elected the different officials of those different branches. In many ways the conflicts between the different branches of our government are a direct result of the conflicts that exist among citizens. Only because of the two-party system is there any efficiency at all. The two parties are able to bridge the gap that is reflected in the ongoing conflict over our dispersal of power among many democratically elected institutions.

This role of parties in our government would have shocked those who wrote the Constitution. The Founders of this country had at best an ambivalent attitude toward parties, and most hoped that parties would not develop into powerful institutions. Despite the fact that deep divisions over political principles, similar to those mentioned earlier, arose very early in our nation's history, many did not believe that permanent parties would emerge. George Washington, for one, refused throughout his career to associate with any party organization, and in his final address to the nation he once again read the traditional indictment against parties:

> It [political parties] serves always to distract the Public Councils and enfeeble the Public Administration. It agitates the Community with ill-founded jealousies and false claims, kindles the animosity of one part against another, foments occasionally riot and insurrection. It opens the door to foreign influence and corruption, which finds a facilitated access to the government itself through the channels of party passion.[9]

Washington's rhetoric was typical of the day; even Jefferson, the architect of the nation's party politics, remarked that if he "could not go to heaven but with party," he "would not go there at all."[10] One can glimpse, in these criticisms and fears, the typical judgments that find parties wanting. The first criticism was that parties divide, rather than unite, us. Furthermore, divisions that already exist in society are accentuated by party factions. Parties, because they create pressures on politicians and separate institutional loyalties, tend to weaken the power of government. Or, as Washington said, parties are inclined to "enfeeble the Public Administration." One hears echoes of this criticism even in the present day.

Washington's concern about weak administration and more recent complaints about gridlock force us to think about the very structure of our government. The desire of the Founders to foster democracy and freedom meant that American needed a system of checks and balances. The benefit of such a system would be that it was responsive to the people, but, by the fact that it had three branches, it would not be too responsive to the immediate, passionate whims of the majority. The United States, unlike many other democracies, has three very distinct and independent ruling powers: the presidency, Congress, and the Supreme Court. While such distinctions were not entirely novel, the Founders developed important nuances in writing the Constitution that meant each of these branches of government would jealously guard its own power and this would make government tyranny unlikely. Conflict between branches is the norm, and the blessed result is that our government is responsive to the demands of the people yet still maintains the ideal of freedom. Thus, to give one example—and unlike many European powers—the executive branch does not arise from the national legislature. It was this very sense of independence that the Founders found most crucial. As James Madison, one of the key authors of the Constitution, wrote:

> In order to lay a due foundation for that separate and distinct exercise of the different powers of government, which to a certain extent is admitted on all hands to be essential to the preservation of liberty, it is evident that each department should have a will of its own; and consequently should have little agency as possible in the appointment of the members of the others. Were the principle rigorously adhered to, it would require that all appointments for the supreme executive, legislature, and judiciary magistracies should be drawn from the same fountain of authority, the people . . .[11]

Of course, we must be careful when we think about what the independence of each branch means. The system of checks and balances gave the different branches independence from each other in the sense that each could justly claim to represent the people. (Or, in the case of the Supreme Court—thought to be the least dangerous branch—justices could claim to be defenders of the Constitution. Hamilton, interestingly enough, thought that the Supreme Court would reflect the public's true, or informed, will.) However, the system also created the real need to share power. Each branch had separate sources of power, and yet only by cooperating could they effectively rule. For laws to be enacted, they must be passed by Congress, approved by the president, and found acceptable by the Supreme Court. To define a public agenda and create policies, each branch would have to work together. This meant each branch would need the other branch, but each would be skeptical of the others. Thus, Madison added: "But the great security against a gradual concentration of the several powers in the same department, consists in giving to those who administer each department the necessary constitutional means and personal motives to resist encroachments of all others."[12] In this way, each individual politician can reasonably claim that he or she speaks for the people. Representatives and senators all assert that they respond to the demands of their constituents; the president makes that claim as well. In a sense, all of them are right. Congressman X speaks for the ninth district and the citizens of that district deserve to be heard; a senator claims to be the champion of opinion in his or her state; finally, the president is emphatic in his ability to voice the demands of the entire nation.

All elected officials, in other words, can make a reasonable claim that they represent their constituents. The problem is that citizens belong to multiple constituencies, and each person makes different demands, depending upon the electoral setting. At the same time officials also have different agendas and these agendas are a function of the institution in which they serve. Congressman see politics from the perspective of a member of the House of Representatives. This means that they feel certain political pressures that senators don't, such as the need to face re-election every two years. Thus congressman are often very responsive to the momentary demands of citizens. They always have a finger raised to measure the direction of the political wind. In recent years, for instance, Republicans found it much easier to pass portions of their "Contract with America" through the House. The House is also a larger institution, with many members. To accomplish anything, representatives must work through committees and this makes them concerned with the multitudinous details of only a few policies, unlike senators who are apt to know a little about a lot of things. Finally, and most importantly, congressman are responsible to a small district, with relatively clear demands from the citizens they represent. As Speaker Tip O'Neill was fond of saying, "All politics is local." This sentiment is echoed by the remarks of many other congressmen: "With congressmen, it's all local. Everything is more local—the local post office, the local industry, the local river, the local airport, the local Miami harbor. Why, if I could get the money to deepen the Miami harbor from fourteen to twenty-one feet, that alone would come damn near to getting me re-elected."[13] If members of the House of Representatives see politics from one point of view, senators see life from a different perspective. Senators, who may be representing larger and more diverse states, feel pressure from more groups and individuals. And senators and congressman are all members of the same branch of government! To add to the potential for disagreement, we must remember that policies are proposed, shaped, and implemented by the executive branch, headed by the president. The president faces other pressures that are bound to make him or her skeptical of congressional action. He was elected in a different manner than the legislators with whom he must work, and he must consider the demands of his own supporters, his administration, the pressure of world events, and, finally, the judgment of history. To complicate politics further, the Supreme Court stands watch over such matters with an attentive demand that constitutional precedents are respected.

What this results in is a continual, intense conflict between the different branches of government, and, since all of these branches have a role in shaping policy, the system moves fitfully, if at all. It takes great effort to get so many people in different institutions of government to agree to anything. As many critics point out, the system is created with numerous veto points, and it requires the persistence and faith of Job to guide deliberations to a conclusion. Politicians must work together to pass legislation and all sides must be consulted. In debates between governmental branches, different constituents are represented and all major perspectives are considered, painstaking compromise on any policy will finally emerge. Gridlock, the favorite political bogeyman of the early 1990s is the intentional design of the founding fathers. The reason is that a regime designed thusly would be democratic, yet still free, because the government would act cautiously when it acted at all.

This system of checks and balances is only the first method used to ensure our political goals. The Founders had another political innovation in mind to guarantee stable, representative democracy: federalism. The different states continue to exist and have great power. One needs only to think about the recent 1996 presidential campaign, with Bob Dole's persistent reference to the Tenth Amendment of the Constitution, to remember that the power of the federal government is not absolute. It is this very thing that Lowi finds so misfortunate: "For one thing, the established parties contribute to the status quo in government structure. For example, they helped maintain the centrality of federalism, even as the national government and the Constitution expanded to meet the problems of a nationally integrated country."

This charge ignores both the vitality of federalism in American politics and the certainty that the states are here to stay. Recent Supreme Court decisions such as *Printz v. United States*, along with the latest welfare policy reforms, all bolster this claim. Some of the Founders, such as Alexander Hamilton, may have preferred to rid the nation of such strong state governments; however, most of the Founders soon realized that the states were quite simply a necessary part of the American experience. As recent policy reforms indicate, the states are laboratories of democracy, as different states experiment with a wide range of policy initiatives. Furthermore, this could lead to a positive political dividend. Madison and the other Founders understood that a large and diverse country would require keeping the states and developing a system of representation. Representation would necessitate a separation between peo- ple and their leaders. This was key since it would result in the creation of a political elite who could be counted upon to filter the emotional and political beliefs of the masses. (This should not necessarily be taken to mean that an elite class would rule and control matters. Madison certainly expected a kind of natural elite to administer politics. In this sense, he, and most of the Found- ers, were elitists. However, Madison also had faith in the judgment of the people and their ultimate authority.) A national, exclusively representative government in a large state necessarily results in distance, both literal and psychological, between the government and the people.

Think for a moment about the office of the president. The president has a strong say in controlling the executive branches of government. (Although this control is not absolute and the potential for conflict is written into parts of the Constitution—for instance, when the Constitution grants the Senate a significant say in the appointment of cabinet officials.) The independence of the president, supported by many readings of the Constitution and bolstered by historical precedent, is an essential part of our political system. The presi- dent stands above the cabinet and the entire civil service and can command control of the executive branch, a difficult thing to achieve but a logical possi- bility inherent in the office. And while it may be obvious, it bears mentioning that this office is singular. The president, unlike a prime minister in the United Kingdom, is not a first among equals in controlling the executive branch. Thus, it is illustrative to recall the story of Lincoln polling his cabinet about Civil War policy and facing the fact that the vote was 8 to 1 against him. However, Lincoln's vote was the only one that mattered and the one triumphed over the many.

In each of these cases, despite the Founders' intentions, they created the conditions that necessitated a two-party system. The two-party system makes the government work effectively. It does not defeat the purpose of the separa- tion of powers; rather, it decreases the tendency of too much gridlock. Parties are the central institutions that allow the different branches of government to work together. As anyone who observes politics quickly learns, the national political agenda can encompass only a few items at a time.[14] This is a result of the conflict-ridden nature of our system, with its many veto points. Yet the two parties help to make the system overcome, from time to time, this "natu- ral" tendency to do nothing. The Congress is divided by party and this helps to organize the chambers. Party loyalty is assumed on many issues and there is an institutional framework provided by the party, through its leadership and party whips in Congress, that encourage politicians to work together.

Lowi's contention that a third party would make our government more re- sponsive is hard to fathom, given the constitutional arrangements under which we currently live. The emergence of a third party would mean that this system, which moves fitfully at best, would be beset with even more interparty conflict and acrimony. The two parties engage in a fair amount of political conflict. A third party would only add to the number of combatants in the political contest. The only way for a third party to effectively make government more responsive would be if we changed the entire basis of our government and terminated our system of separation of powers. A parliamentary system, in which the executive arises out of the legislature, might work. However, this means we would have to abandon the Constitution (or, at the very least, engage in massive doctrinal surgery). If we failed to do this, the only result would be a less responsive government that gave citizens the illusion of more representation.

Oddly, these criticisms are being made at a time when parties are more effective in articulating political goals and encouraging their members in government to work together to achieve those goals. Recent years have witnessed increased party loyalty among members of Congress. The parties meet in caucus to discuss policies, work out political strategy, and, if necessary, cajole members to think of the greater good that the party represents. The ability of Newt Gingrich to unite the Republican Party behind "The Contract with America" illustrates the value of parties in making the system work. Outside of Congress, parties provide the president with a logical place to turn for allies in passing legislation and developing government programs. Thus, both within Congress and between Congress and the president, political parties create a team that can work to achieve a set of policies. As the presidencies of Andrew Jackson, Abraham Lincoln, Woodrow Wilson, and Franklin Roosevelt clearly reveal, unified party government is able to make our complex government work productively. Conversely, as the Clinton administration's recent problems with congressional Democrats demonstrate, there is no assurance that parties can overcome institutional separation. Political parties are like modern baseball teams: there is a presumption of common effort; however, we can never count on long-term enduring loyalty.

The appeal of party affiliation, as is exemplified in the passage of Clinton's first budget, is that they are the one nongovernmental institution that can link the branches and overcome the natural tendency of the system to grind to a halt. Not one Republican in either the House or the Senate voted for Clinton's first proposed budget. The Democrats, while suffering a few defections, exhibited remarkable support for their president. Our political history tells us this kind of party unity is difficult to maintain; however, it is unlikely that a third party would make such unity any easier to sustain. In fact, the existence of a third party would make it easier for members to defect to a new political team. These potential defections would expand the many veto points that already exist in our system. Thus, the passage of bills through subcommittees, committees, and to the floor of the chamber would become even more difficult with the addition of another party. The two-party system allows occasional unity in government so that policy innovation can be attempted, usually during extraordinary times. A strong third party would most likely weaken the ability of the system to achieve these infrequent, yet vital, moments.

America was destined to have a two-party system. There are more reasons that American politics gravitates toward the two parties: the process of elections.

IV

While many of the Founders exhibited a general hostility toward parties, others expected a kind of multiparty system to emerge. The political system they built would work especially well if, as Madison said, there were numerous different factions and groups. However, so many groups in society would certainly seem to lead to many parties, not a few. Instead, Madison envisioned a cacophony of parties and factions canceling each other's excesses out:

> The smaller the society, the fewer probably will be the distinct parties and interests composing it; the fewer the distinct parties and interests, the more frequently will a majority be found from the same party . . . Extend the sphere, and you take in a greater variety of parties and interests; you make it less probable that a majority of the whole will have a common motive to invade the rights of other citizens.[15]

In this desire to foster the ideal of liberty over the strict demands of democracy, Madison envisioned numerous parties representing the radically different groups that compose the American nation.

Yet it was this very expectation of numerous parties that was so quickly thwarted by the design the government adopted. Madison helped to lead the way, with his ally and mentor Thomas Jefferson, by creating an opposition party. The early Republican Party (not to be confused with the present-day party of that name) embodied the necessity of the two-party system. For starters, it reminds us that the two-party system is likely because of the presumption that some politicians will organize and oppose those in power. Thus, every position creates a contrary position. However, Madison's ideas about parties offer greater lessons about the importance of two parties. Madison was drawn to the two-party system as a necessity for accountable, mass democratic politics. This is especially true because each of the two parties were bound to be a coalition of many factions. Such broad-based coalitional parties did not fully contradict Madison's ideas about the need for many factions. Happily, the two-party system preserved many of the benefits of a large, diversified, factional nation that Madison envisioned, and it helped to create a viable, unified opposition force—something Madison keenly appreciated when he went into opposition. This also made parties the key factor in maintaining stability and democracy. To understand this remarkable outcome, we need to consider the process of elections created by the Founders and developed over time in the nation.

Despite the importance of elite control over politics, the Founders did envision some democratic influence. This influence would primarily be felt through the election process, and this election process itself bolstered the creation of the two-party system. Of course, as many commentators on politics like to point out, single-member districts tend to create two-party systems.[16] (The American experience provides one important complication to this idea. For over one hundred years in the South, America had a one-party system. This was largely the result of the wrenching turmoil of the Civil War. Still, single-member districts were used in most cases and no third parties emerged. Political conflict was pushed back to the Democratic primary.) The logic is that without proportional representation, there must be one winner in each district. Proportional representation can come in slightly different forms; however, the main idea is that parties are represented in government in a way that reflects the number of votes they received, even if no party garners a majority. Thus, there might be a ten-member district in which Party X receives 40 percent of the vote, Party Y 30 percent, Party Z 30 percent. In this case, Party X will have four representatives, Party Y three representatives, and Party Z three members in government. Thus, there are several winners from every district. Although this method is perfectly legal and has been used from time to time in this country, it is not the dominant form of representation.

Under the conditions of single-member district with only one winner, the tendency is for all opposition to coalesce around one challenger. Why waste your vote and needlessly divide the opposition? In a single-member district, opposition parties will thus, over time, unite to oppose the majority party candidate. American voters tend to be rational people who can calculate the odds of their candidate winning and will make a reasonable decision about the lesser of two evils. Although some voters stubbornly vote for third parties—to make a statement or because winning is unimportant to them—most voters reward the two major parties with support. The Founders would certainly recognize this possibility with the direct election of the members of the House of Representatives. However, we should admit that this could easily lead to each district creating its own two-party system—thus, we could imagine a two-party system repeated 435 times over or various larger regional differences. Single-member districts do not necessarily create a two-party system; they merely create the probability of bifactional conflicts in many different places. What could possibly compel a *national* two-party system? The answer is found in the lure of the presidency and the way this man or woman is selected. Furthermore, this factor shows us that moving to a system of proportional representation would only be the first step in creating a multiparty system.

The presidency is selected via the electoral college. This is another example of the Founders' distrust of direct democracy and their faith in elite influence. Despite their intentions, this institution created two parties. To see why this is the case, we need to review how the electoral college works. Each state is assigned electors on the basis of the size of each state's delegation to Congress. This means that larger states receive more electoral votes; however, smaller states are guaranteed at least three votes (each state has at least one representative and two senators). Furthermore, each state can decide how it selects its electors. (Although today all states use some method of popular selection of electors.) The president would not be chosen directly by the people; rather, the selection process filters the opinions of citizens. The resulting system means that when people vote, they actually vote for a slate of electors who are, in practice, pledged to vote for a certain presidential candidate.[17]

If no candidate receives a majority of the electoral college votes (there are 538, thus a majority is 270) then the choice of president falls on the House of Representatives, where the members of the House act, with each state delegation voting to cast its one state ballot. Consequently, this rather complicated system would require that a candidate receive the support of a majority of states to win the election. Although this has only happened once, in 1824, and never in this century, the electoral college exists to this day. Furthermore, it has a tremendous effect upon the political process. Campaigns are geared toward winning 270 electoral votes and candidates spend inordinate amounts of time canvassing for votes in California, the state richest in electoral votes, with 54. Although there is a slight variation in how states award their electoral college votes, most simply allow that whoever receives a plurality of votes cast gets all the electoral votes. Thus, some candidates, such as Ross Perot in 1992, garner considerable support among the electorate but receive no support in the electoral college. Many question the fairness of this system, but it was the intention of the Founders to limit too much direct democracy and the electoral college has its defenders to this day. In practice, it may be true that all presidential candidates since 1888 have received a majority of the electoral college votes and a plurality of the popular votes cast, but there is no need for the latter to occur. It is quite possible for a candidate to win a combination of states, totaling 270 electoral votes, and not even be on the ballot in every other state. The result would most likely be a president who received a clear minority of votes cast. To the Founders this may be an unfortunate, but hardly tragic, occurrence. However, to contemporary ears this sounds undemocratic and dashes our expectations that the choice of the president reflects the majority of American voters.

What the Founders didn't anticipate was the national nature of two parties contesting the presidency. Our present system of selecting the president was amended after the 1800 election. As we have noted, George Washington and other early leaders of the Republic detested parties and expected a less partisan, and more consensual, method of selecting the president. However, the immediate emergence of a party of opposition led to controversy in the 1800 election. By pulling the various local parties together into an effective opposition, Jefferson was able to win the election. Members of the electoral college voted once for president and once for vice president. The problem was that under the system used, whoever received a majority of the electoral votes became president. A hero such as Washington created no problems for the system—he simply received a clear majority of the votes. In a partyless world, the vice president was the next most popular leader, among a likely scattering of ballots. However, in a world where parties are emerging, the vice-president could be of a differing party than the president. This is precisely what happened in 1796, when John Adams, a nominal Federalist, won the presidency and Thomas Jefferson, a leader of the Republican Party, received the second most votes and was elected vice president.

This problem was accentuated in the election of 1800. In that election, the Republican ticket of Jefferson-Burr defeated the Federalists Adams and Pickney. Since the Constitution did not recognize parties, Jefferson's running mate, Aaron Burr, ending up receiving the same number of votes as Jefferson. The election was thrown into the House of Representatives, and it took thirty-five ballots to resolve and spare the nation the threat of a Burr presidency. This confusion led to the Twelfth Amendment to the Constitution, which now recognizes presidential and vice presidential votes in the electoral college. This amendment enshrined the two-party system, since we assume that the president and the vice president should be members of the same party.

Even without this amendment, the nature of the party system was changing the way we looked at the presidential election. The electoral vote of a state does not have to be decided on a winner-take-all basis. However, the rise of the two-party system and the need to democratically elect the president eventually fostered this. Despite the intention of the Founders, the need for a president selected by the parties pulled us toward a two-party system. Third parties tend toward less impressive showings in the electoral college. Despite the fact that Ross Perot received almost 20 percent of the popular vote in 1992, he received no electoral college votes. Third parties that win electoral college votes tend to be regional, like George Wallace's in 1968—heavily concentrated in one section of the country. However, such geographic concentration robs the third party of any realistic chance of victory. Thus, third parties tend to have their support either diffused throughout the country, which results in no electoral college support, or concentrated in one region, which means that such candidates can make no claim for a national appeal. If a third party emerges that wants to win the presidency—and most strong examples of third parties focus their energies on winning this office—it is necessary to create the conditions that make this a realistic possible. To conceive the possibility of a viable third party, it would be imperative that we eliminate the electoral college. This would strike at the heart of the Constitution and the principle of Federalism. The states still matter, as the electoral college reminds us. Furthermore, as Judith Best forcefully argues, the electoral college does an excellent job in providing us with a clear and swift decision for the presidency.[18] The two parties, by splitting the electoral college votes between them, give us a clear winner on election night. A strong third party would rob us of such electoral clarity.

V

The reasons given thus far—the dual principles of American politics, the nature of government, and the ability of parties to organize elections—are all reasons that suggest two parties would emerge as they did. As it stands, I think this should make us realize how unlikely the possibility is that an effective third party could ever emerge. Some people want a third party and that might be a good thing; however, American politics creates all sorts of roadblocks and makes such a party unlikely.

Still, that does not end our debate about third parties. After all, significant reform might create the conditions sufficient to build an effective third party. We must now turn to reasons that tell us that a two-party system is a positive good for our politics. Given the American desire for more political choices and the general national faith in the power of reform, I would like to convince critics of the two-party system that American politics is improved by the present party system. And, as we mentioned earlier, there are three reasons to be grateful that we have only two parties. The first reason flows out of the way we conduct elections.

The two-party system makes the election process clear and increases the possibility of useful democratic accountability. An effective third party would muddle the selection of the president. Such a party, if it won any significant number of electoral votes, would defer to the House of Representatives. Such an eventuality would certainly be in line with what the Founders expected. However, their main goal was to limit mass participation in the selection of the president. The rise of mass democracy makes the president a key figure in the relationship between government and citizens. This is the result of the presidential election process, which gives the president legitimacy because success requires that millions of Americans come together to elect a leader. It is also true that the electoral college discourages third parties and, in so doing, the election usually produces a president who receives a majority of the popular votes. The only thing that third parties can do, in the present system, is to rob a president of a likely majority vote and diminish the possibilities of a mandate. More than one commentator links many of the Clinton presidency's shortcomings to his receiving only 42 percent of the popular vote in the 1992

election, less than a majority vote. The elimination of the electoral college
would result in this circumstance being the norm: either the president would
receive only a plurality of the votes or it would be necessary to hold a run-off
election.

If that was not enough, a third party would actually weaken democracy
by undermining the mechanism of accountability. The ability to hold leaders
accountable is a central part of a fully functioning democracy, and the two-
party system makes accountability relatively clear. The two-party system simplifies giving credit and assigning blame. The president is a model in this
regard. Coalition, cabinet government makes it very difficult for the average
voter to clearly censure or commend leaders. This is probably unfair to leaders, since it simplifies matters too much; however, it is a necessity in a nation
where voters are fundamentally distant from, and not directly involved in,
government. At the very least, a two-party system allows voters to vote against
an administration or candidate—a crucial chance to express frustration for
voters who never hold direct power themselves. If we are not going to allow
voters to act directly in politics, it is incumbent for a democracy to give them
a clear opportunity to apportion blame. This is the minimum, necessary, type
of accountability that is created in a two-party system.

Despite complaints about the similarities between the Republicans and
Democrats, Americans increasingly see significant differences between the
two parties. Although this is never easy and there is still a great deal of confusion, most Americans can identify the "conservative" party and the "liberal"
party. George Wallace's observation that there was not a "dime's worth of
difference" between the two parties rings less and less true.[19] As the midterm
elections of 1994 confirmed, citizens can assign blame and take action accordingly. A multiparty system would make this relationship very confusing.
Some argue that much of the frustration in contemporary politics springs from
divided government, where all politicians can successfully run against Washington and the other party. In the world of divided government each politician
can essentially blame the other party—which controls the other branch of
government—for whatever failures exist. Despite the persistence of divided
government, the two-party system allows for the possibility of unified government, some of the time. A multiparty system would almost certainly preclude
this possibility altogether. The result might be politicians who could run
against Washington in every election. Since no one party is ever in control,
no one politician can ever be held responsible. Of course, this happens today;
however, there is no reason to encourage this deplorable tendency among politicians. The recent confusion of divided government could only be exacer-
bated by the emergence of another party.

VI

Another reason we should be thankful that we only have two parties is a cultural one. Political parties engage in cultural bridging that is crucial in a land

as diverse as America. The two-party system requires parties to forge coalitions, not just in Washington, but among citizens. It is the unique role of parties as associations that matters most and this role is highlighted by the consideration of what a third party would entail. Political parties are essential actors in creating a civil society that helps overcome our divisions. At their best, parties create unity—or, at least, tolerable cooperation—among groups that would rather not work with anyone else. This is the parties' special mandate, and by uniting the diversity they make citizens realize that we need each other more, an essential lesson for democracies.

Parties are the preeminent example of civic associations. As Tocqueville observed, Americans are traditionally a nation of joiners—we join service clubs, business clubs, hobby groups, and political parties. Over a hundred and fifty years ago Tocquevile described America as a land of individuals; however, this individualism was tempered by a strong desire to join others and form groups.

> Civil associations, therefore, facilitate political associations; but, on the other hand, political association singularly strengthens and improves associations for civil purposes. In civil life every man may, strictly speaking, fancy that he can provide for his own wants; in politics he can fancy no such thing. When a people, then, have any knowledge of public life, the notion of association and the wish to coalesce present themselves every day to the minds of the whole community; whatever natural repugnance may restrain men from acting in concert, they will always be ready to combine for the sake of party. Thus, political life makes the love and practice of association more general; it imparts a desire of union and teaches the means of combination to numbers of men who otherwise would have always lived apart.[20]

One of the most powerful examples of this kind of civic action was the creation of the great political parties. They are a special form of civil association, dedicated to drawing lesser associations together into a majority coalition. They teach people about politics and supply a sense of identity and political bonding that connects citizens and their leaders. They also create bonds among different sets of leaders. In this sense they encourage civility at all levels of politics, precisely because they force their constituent groups to respect each other and to moderate dogma in the interest of accommodation. This difficult goal is achieved at the expense of limiting pure representation of all the divergent political perspectives and the complete diversity of American civic life. A third party, which could open the door for many more parties, would start us down the road to making political parties just like any other sectarian or narrowly interested group. The distinctive quality that makes the two parties more than just another set of interest groups would be lost.

As Robert Putnam has pointed out in his recent research, Americans are no longer so likely to join associations—political or otherwise.[21] Americans are bowling alone, as Putnam tells us, and increasingly they are voting and acting politically as individuals and not as members of a political party. More and more, our lives are lived in private places and in isolation. Americans gather news about life at home via television and, increasingly, the Internet, which frequently requires people to stay at home. Much recent sociological research reveals that Americans live in communities that are not very diverse.[22] However, the nation as whole is very diverse. The mass media and the suburbs contribute to this. We select television programs that reflect who we are, and we live in communities of people of the same color and with startlingly similar income levels.[23] Americans are likely to live in what Robert Bellah calls "life style enclaves"—in suburbs of cities—of people who are very alike (even if our relationships are often transient and superficial). This means we are no longer required to see other people, to interact with people who are different from us. This sort of privatized individual liberty is virtually the opposite of self-government. Democracy is not about being free from politics, it is about being free to engage *in* politics. Yet when we engage *in* politics, we interact with people who are vastly different from us, who have different ideals and different ways of seeing the world.

The two-party system is the last hope for the maintenance of civil society—which even the Founders acknowledged was necessary for the success of the American experiment in self-government. By becoming a member of a party, a person becomes part of a greater and more enduring institution that demands something of that individual. Even just "joining" a party via semi-loyal voting patterns can remind individuals of their connections to other citizens. Democracy requires us to accept others and to work with them. A civil society is one that is just that, civil enough to get along. It requires us to interact and prove our civility in an ongoing process. We need institutions, like political parties, that encourage people to work together for common goals. Part of Lowi's appeal is his fervent belief that American politics needs to be revitalized. I share his genuine concerns, yet I do not think the solution is found in scuttling the traditional party system; instead, we should look for ways to strengthen it. We agree, in large measure, about the ills that affect American politics. However, the cure offered is significantly different. At the very moment in our history when we need institutions that encourage us to work together politically, more parties would splinter us into even more factions.

The two-party system provides a set of institutions that makes people of vastly different experiences come together. How can one look at a Democratic convention, with its Southern moderates, feminists, socially conservative/economically liberal union leaders, gay activists, and Californians and not realize the diversity of America and the Democratic Party? Yet if we begin to create a multiparty system these groups would most likely separate. Of course, as any Democrat would tell us, it is hard enough to unite all these groups, and the modern Democratic Party would have been impossible without Franklin Roosevelt's extraordinary leadership, which enabled him, and the Democratic

Party, to change American politics. The same things can be said about Ronald Reagan's leadership of the Republican Party. He was able to unify social and economic conservatives to redefine politics in the 1980s. On the surface, the Republican Convention reveals a more uniform picture. The party is obviously whiter and wealthier than the Democratic Party. However, this outward sign of similarity hides the great diversity that exists in a party that includes libertarians, evangelicals, social conservatives, and technophilic entrepreneurs. But Reagan's coalition, like Roosevelt's, was framed by the necessity of two-party politics.

Representing all the diversity of American life is important in making democracy work, but democracy also requires a reflection of our likeness and commonality, the great principle of civic equality. It presumes a government that is accountable and one that enables different people to work together. The public good demands that we recognize something that is common along with our apparent differences. The two political parties do just that, while allowing a lively debate about what goals Americans should cherish above all else. It is revealing that neither party has ever been too dominant for too long because the spirit of American life requires a tension between the Republican call for individual liberty and the Democratic belief in equality. Possibly the two-party system is disliked for this very reason. It reminds us that this conflict lies at the heart of our politics. The multiparty system would transform this tension into something more divisive, lessening the pressure to search for coalitions and common good. Americans need the two-party system to keep the debate of America going and then to keep this debate from spinning out of control. It is certainly true that the two-party system has flaws, and I am not alone in my belief that it often fails to do the things I wish it would. However, its success is more likely than any other method we have yet imagined.

VII

There is one final reason that should make us leery of any effort to create a viable third party. American political history is defined by a two-party system and, although there have been significant challenges to this dominance from time to time, third parties have never flourished. To create a third party would require important and extensive reforms to the political process. Although Lowi puts his faith in a series of court challenges that would change our understanding of representation and the way we select congressmen, recent Supreme Court decisions indicate that the present Court prefers the two-party system. (The most recent case, *Timmons v. Twin Cities Area New Party*, upholds the ability of the government to discourage third parties by banning fusion tickets. Fusion tickets are a device by which third parties nominate a major party candidate on their ticket. The idea is to use the popularity of a major party nominee to help bolster the appeal of a third party.) It is not a foregone conclusion that the courts will decide as Lowi suggests and legislation will be necessary, not to mention amending the Constitution.

To reconstitute our party system would end or weaken the system of checks and balances that has served us so well for two centuries. We should be cautious in advocating such reforms. The results of such actions would be a tremendous rethinking of American political practice. As Lowi frankly admits:

> Over time, a three-party system would alter the Constitution of the American regime. Very quickly and directly, the entire pattern and recruitment and succession would change. The separation of powers would begin to recede until the presidency and both Houses of Congress had become a single institution.

Lowi believes that the entire foundation of American politics should and will be changed. I disagree that such changes are necessary. Our Founders provided us with an excellent system of government that has successfully adapted to a changing world. This is not to suggest that all is perfect and that reforms are unnecessary. However, reforms should take place within the present system. Our efforts should instead focus on making the two parties better and more effective.

One of the more agonizing factors about political life is that one set of changes often creates unexpected consequences. The American Founders did not expect a two-party system to develop, yet it did. Politics is very complicated and to suggest reforms is to open up a Pandora's box of possibilities. There is an old expression that provides much political wisdom: "Don't take down the fence until you know why it was put up." In addressing those problems, we should act only when the causes of our problems are clear and the solution is likely to be near at hand. The two-party system is not so corrupt that we should abandon it altogether. Furthermore, it is not clear that a third party would do a better job of representing the people or providing us with good and efficient government. A third party would address a symptom of problems without providing a real cure to the maladies that affect the American body politic. In most cases a third party would make the present system even less efficient, reduce accountability, and confuse citizens even more.

VIII

What exactly would a third party do? In most cases it would make American politics worse. There are at least five reasons to be skeptical of a third party. First, what principles would they represent? Third parties have existed from time to time to advocate important ideas and, as such, these parties played a valuable role in American political history. In the late nineteenth century, the Democratic Party, under the leadership of William Jennings Bryan, moved forcefully to capture the appeal of the Populists. Just a few years later, both parties made concerted efforts to tap into the reforming spirit of the Progressive movement. Richard Nixon, in the late 1960s and early 1970s, made a conscious effort to win over the Southern voters who supported George Wallace and his American Independent Party. Finally, most recently, both parties engaged in strenuous efforts to attract the followers of Ross Perot. In each of these cases, the major parties recognized the appeal of the third party candidate and saw the need to extend their coalition and broaden their voter base.

The Populist Party, the Progressive Party, and Ross Perot's Reform Party all had significant influence on the way Americans talked about politics and the issues addressed by leaders in Washington. This ability to affect the national agenda is laudable. However, if there is some overriding dualism in American politics, then a third party would add nothing, *in the long term*, to American politics. In many cases, third parties spring up when the major parties fail to address important issues. (Of course, third parties also emerge to advocate less pleasant ideals. We should not forget the Know-Nothings of the 1840s with their hostility to immigrants, or George Wallace's appeal to racism.) However, the ability to raise and address certain transitory issues is not reason enough to foster a permanent third party. American history tells us that once these issues are raised, one of the two major parties moves to meet the challenge and co-opt the third party's main issues. Thus, Ross Perot and his supporters spoke to the need to deal seriously with the massive budget deficits of the 1980s and 1990s. While this issue is of great significance, it is hard to see why one should create a party to handle such a problem. Budgetary reform, while important, is not in the same philosophical league as personal freedom or social equality. Furthermore, by the end of the decade it is more and more apparent that the two established parties, admittedly prompted by Perot and his supporters, have largely solved the fiscal crisis, at least for the foreseeable future. If we create the conditions necessary for permanent third parties, we risk creating a party that only serves to obfuscate the debate that endures between the two parties.[24]

This leads to the second reason to be leery of a third party—the issue of accountability. Third parties would confuse Americans even more about who is in control in Washington and who to credit or blame. Since most Americans take only a passing interest in politics, the two parties provide a running scorecard that simplifies, without making meaningless, the ongoing political battles fought by political leaders.[25] If we all were interested in politics all the time, we might not need parties. But America was dedicated to the idea of freedom, democratic politics, and that means we need to be free from politics, *some of the time*. Accountability is relatively easily maintained in a two-party system in which citizens have a cursory interest in politics. Many citizens use parties as a key voting cue and their party loyalty runs no deeper than a general predisposition to vote for one of the parties. In this sense, citizens don't have to follow politics too closely to make reasonable voting decisions. A multi-party system would most likely require of a citizen constant political vigilance to learn who is responsible for which government action. Such vigilance would certainly be a good thing. However, it is not likely that a third party would, in the long run, actually encourage such citizen interest in politics. Even if it raised levels of participation, the participation would be more confusing and less thoughtful.

Third, a permanent third party would certainly weaken the presidency because it would increase the likelihood that the House of Representatives would select the president. A strong third party might frequently win enough electoral votes to guarantee that no candidate received the 270 necessary to win. This is not the norm in American politics. Furthermore, Americans have historically not been content when presidential elections were unclear. I would also be skeptical of the intrigue that would result from the House making a decision about the presidency—a decision that was previously reserved for the American people. Over time the third party might force us to consider abandoning the electoral college, and this could further confuse the way we select our president. A third party, without an electoral college, would mean either a series of plurality presidents or would necessitate a run-off election. The last thing this country needs is another round of expansive elections.

Fourth, another party would actually increase gridlock, instead of reducing this problem. Imagine for a moment that a third party won the presidency or significant seats in the Congress. The failures of Richard Nixon and Jimmy Carter attest to the difficulties of presidents who circumvent the party system, and these leaders at least had some affiliation with the two major parties. The possibility of gridlock would increase even further with a strong third party. Even if the third party won just a few seats in Congress, it could slow the process of government even more. The ability to coordinate activity between government branches and internal branch action would be compromised. The ability to engage in "horsetrading" to get things done will happen in any political system; however, the two parties facilitate this process and make it more likely that fellow party members engage in successful bargaining. The formation of the party caucus in Congress creates an institution that can help coordinate the activity of members and encourage them to work together as a legislative team—even if only fitfully. The parties also provide a president with allies in Congress, whom he can usually count upon for help. To some this may be unseemly, but it is absolutely essential in making government work. To critics such as Lowi, the possibility of gridlock is diminished by a third party, but that is because the very idea of separation of powers and federalism is rendered meaningless. Not only is this unlikely, but it is positively dangerous to engage in wholesale reforms necessary to accomplish this.

Finally, a third party would significantly weaken the role of cultural bridging that does occur within the two parties. The two parties force people to work together, even if they don't want to. They also force people to moderate their demands. The complex coalitions that define the Democrats and Republicans represent institutions that foster bonds between remarkably disparate groups. It is likely that once we start down the road to a third party, more parties are sure to follow. Lowi, of course, only wants one more party, but once that happened, it would be harder and harder to force people to compromise in the name of party. Given the incredible diversity in American life, it would not be surprising that more and more groups would begin to demand their own parties and start working toward that goal. The different groups that make up the Democratic coalition might easily attempt to form their own parties. The Republicans face very similar problems.

IX

If, as I have suggested, a third party would not solve our political problems, what would help? The answer lies in making the parties we have today more effective. However, the issue of effectiveness raises some very important questions about what is most important in our democracy, particularly the issue of representation, which is so central to this debate. Your opinion about representation will determine the number of parties you feel are necessary.

One function of parties is to represent the people in government. They are the vital connection between citizens and their government. But what does it mean to represent and how does this connection work? If to represent we merely want to re-present all the diversity that exists in the larger world, then government should reflect American society on a smaller scale. Congress would be the United States in miniature and we could select Congress (even the president) by a lottery. If such a proposal is too disturbing, then a multiparty system offers a way to represent more of the diversity found in America.

However, for the Founders representation meant something quite different. Leaders would represent constituents, but not directly. This means that leaders should not simply parrot the views of their constituents—if that was the case, we could easily have a national referendum on issues. Instead, they represent the concerns and beliefs of citizens, but they also filter them through the act of coming together and deliberating in Congress. In fact, in the very act of re-electing a member of Congress, the public comes to some judgment about a politician's entire record, for the whole term. This in itself means that the citizens must consider an individual's abilities, membership on key committees, the persuasive skills of that member, and not consider issues taken singularly. (Although, of course, there are always some voters who consider only one issue to be pertinent.) The entire process is designed to limit the extent to which Congress or the president simply represent the entirety of opinions of the populace. As James Madison wrote, representation would change our notions of the public good, because it would:

> refine and enlarge and public views, by passing them through a medium of a chosen body of citizens, whose wisdom may best discern the true interest of their country, whose patriotism and love of justice will be least likely to sacrifice it to temporary or partial considerations. Under such a regulation, it may well happen that the public voice, pronounced by the representatives of the people, will be more consonant to the public good than if pronounced by the people themselves, convened for the purpose.[26]

This ideal can be justified on two different grounds. To some (including many of the founding fathers) representatives would frankly include the best of our nation. Such an idea is clearly elitist. However, to others, representatives are not so much better than the average citizen than they are *different*, because they are members of a unique institution. You could take almost any citizen and put her in the U.S. Congress and she would begin to act, in some degree, as Madison suggests. The responsibilities in fulfilling the role of representative will transform most people. By either theory, though, the very act of creating a system of representation modifies the will of the people. Governments must be responsive to the people they represent, but they must not be subservient to the momentary whims of the citizens. Oddly enough, despite a perverse fascination with polling (read any copy of *USA Today*), people often complain that today's politicians follow the latest polling results too closely. On reflection, this apparently indicates a native distrust of too much democracy. Assuming that polls are conducted carefully, this seems to say that Americans don't always trust themselves.

Yet we know that Americans believe in democracy and are capable of some kind of self-rule. The issue that we must consider is how this filtering process of representation can best occur. How do we balance the desire for popular control and the belief that we need good government? The Founders were much more elitist and critical of democracy than we are today. However, they certainly created the possibility for a degree of democratic control. With the rise of mass political parties, there was an increase in participation and, furthermore, government became more directly accountable to the people.

From the end of the eighteenth century through the early part of the nineteenth century, suffrage was greatly restricted. However, as the last century progressed, more and more restrictions on voting were lifted, so that the country soon had something close to universal suffrage for white men. What this meant was that parties were no longer simply the institutional creatures of a select few national and state leaders. More and more people were voting and states were, for instance, making the electoral college reflect the will of this larger electorate. The democratic impulse of American life was real and making itself felt, via the institution of national parties. Increasingly, parties organized and mobilized voters and this meant that they were the integral force in fostering political participation. It was certainly still true that most Americans could not be involved in the day-to-day operation of government. The size of the nation and the time it took to travel to state capitals precluded direct involvement on the part of citizens. However, the selection of those who set policy was increasingly the result of elections in which a very high percentage of citizens participated. After much change and evolution, a stable two-party system emerged by the time of the Civil War. Thus, the parties created the vital connection of accountability between citizens and leaders.

These two parties did wonders in encouraging men (and, later, women) to vote and they raised participation rates to record levels. Often political scientists lament the low rate of voting among Americans, which is usually contrasted with the routinely high turnouts of 70–90 percent exhibited by European democracies. In the most recent presidential election in this country, less than 50 percent of eligible voters bothered to cast a ballot. Participation in "off-year" congressional and local races is even worse—usually less than 40 percent of eligible voters. However, Americans did turn out in impressive numbers in the past. But for critics of the two-party system, the disturbing news is that such levels of participation developed under the careful care of the great party machines run by the two parties. We are likely to think of urban parties such as Tammany Hall of New York, or the Pendergast Machine of Kansas City, or Mayor Daley and the Cook County Democratic Party, but party organizations were just as strong—and just as questionable—around rural and small town courthouses. Nonetheless, no matter how reviled, such institutions have been closely correlated with high rates of voter participation, one of the hallmarks of democracy. It was the two-party system and the strong organizations of the mid-nineteenth to the mid-twentieth century that helped inaugurate mass, representative democracy.

However, critics of the two-party system might point out that participation would probably rise with more parties. In fact, there is some evidence for this point of view. In 1992 a well-funded third candidate helped to raise voter turnout. (Of course, three choices in 1996 did not help much.) Simply put, a third party would mean more activists and more party workers and this might very well increase participation rates. One of the functions of a political party is to mobilize voters, and more parties would increase the ability of the system to encourage voting. However, this is not the only goal we are trying to foster. The challenge for American politics is how to balance the laudable goal of high levels of participation with an effective and good government. American political history confirms that it was the two-party system in the nineteenth century that was able to reasonably meet both of these demands.

This dilemma encourages us to reflect upon the way Americans have historically thought about government and their leaders. In a large nation of diverse peoples that relies on representative government, one of the greatest dangers is that government will be seen as distant, uncaring, and unresponsive. This problem was real in the nineteenth century and is even more true today. Much polling data shows that people don't trust their government and the ideas of many of the militia movements are only the most extreme expression of this suspicion. In the past, the two parties helped to overcome this threat of distance. The political parties were rooted in local organizations and relied upon the explicit power of face-to-face campaigning. This ideal is of supreme importance in the development of democracy. As George Washington Plunkitt observed:

> There's only one way to hold a district: you must study human nature and act accordin'. To learn real human nature you have to go among the people, see them and be seen. I know every man, woman, and child in the Fifteenth District, except them that's been born this summer—and I know some of them, too.[27]

In this very real sense, the traditional party system created something akin to political friendship among citizens.[28] Plunkitt's great success was built upon the knowledge that he knew his constituents and, just as important, they knew something of him. Although this is always a difficult relationship to maintain in a large society, America was a sizable and diversified nation in the last century and parties were able to overcome the separation between citizens and leaders.

The danger is that distance will create other, more dangerous, attitudes about politics. By making the connection between government and the people more real and effective, parties serve an essential function in the system. The Founders may not have realized this, but parties actually served to make the system more stable by making government seem more real and personal. Alexander Hamilton argued that government should have a direct effect upon the people:

> It [the federal government] must stand in need of no intermediate legislations; but must itself be empowered to employ the arm of the ordinary magistrate to execute its own resolutions. . . . The government of the Union, like that of each State, must be able to address itself immediately to the hopes and fears of individuals.[29]

But in a country growing more democratic, it is also essential that government be touched by the people. This was the supreme accomplishment of the party system. Political parties enabled leaders to communicate and guide citizens, and they enabled citizens to hold leaders accountable and to assign credit and blame as the citizens saw fit.

The two parties did that with a fair amount of proficiency. The party system that developed in the nineteenth century was dedicated to fostering mass participation and making our government work. Why was that the case? What role did parties perform that made them so dear to the political process and why were they successful in bringing people to the polls? First of all, parties were the great purveyors of political information. Americans may not be able to comprehend this in today's world of television, the Internet, and whatever new lanes of communication are constructed in cyberspace; however, in the nineteenth century and a good part of this century, news about politics was spread via the party. There were ward leaders, party rallies, and meetings that all served to educate the public. Alongside these explicit party activities, most newspapers were closely aligned with one of the major political parties— much more so than the intermittent endorsements we see today. This was an essential function of parties and one that is largely gone today. Today, newspapers are more likely to claim political neutrality and are certainly less important than television as a source of information. While certain television shows include clear ideological perspectives, such programs are usually not the sole source of information and these commentators are not directly linked to either political party in an official capacity.

Second, parties were a great source of jobs. Patronage was an essential aspect of the party's power and a source of their appeal to voters. "To the victor goes the spoils" was the famous slogan from the last century. Although this cry sounds corrupt to contemporary ears, it was embraced in the last century by staunch supporters of democracy. When one party won an election, they were entitled to reward their followers with jobs—and even today that is what an election is partially about. (Although this practice is less prevalent now, I can still remember hearing about a local New Jersey party leader who declared that after the election, jobs would be distributed by the following criteria: (1) The best jobs would go to local party members who worked for the recent slate of candidates; (2) next in line were other party members who showed less marked enthusiasm; (3) any jobs left over would go to people on the basis of competence. And this was in the late 1980s!) When one side wins an election, that means they get to run the government. There was never an abundance of jobs to go around, but any job was important and had a ripple effect throughout the community. Even those who did not get a position might know someone who did. The idea of a neutral civil service is largely a twentieth century idea.

The third function of parties is educational. Parties are teachers of democracy—even the corrupt machines of days past taught a valuable lesson to new Americans. They taught people that their votes mattered. It may be true that at some level citizens were bribed, cajoled, and even threatened into voting; still, this act of voting was clearly important and was considered a resource. If the machines used methods we are uncomfortable with today, they still taught a fundamental first lesson in American democracy—every vote counts (at least once). Besides, we are apt to overestimate the power of the political machines; their candidates were overthrown at the ballot box from time to time and, even more often, they lost elections involving wider electorates. This meant that citizens could witness the peaceful transfer of power, another basic lesson of democracy.

All these activities took place within the confines of a two-party world. Government became more responsive to citizens via the two parties, while at the same time Madison's ideas about a "refined and enlarged" leadership that makes for good representation was maintained. The ability of parties to do all these things, however, was radically changed in the twentieth century. We must now turn to this development and see how and why these changes took place. In so doing, we shall see how the parties evolved. As the parties changed, they created new problems and challenges for American politics. Yet these problems do not suggest we need more parties. Rather, we must make the two parties stronger.

X

Despite the positive case that two parties were effective promoters of representative democracy, there is no denying that parties in the late nineteenth century failed in many ways to efficiently and ethically represent the people. These concerns led to the rise of the Progressive movement. While some Progressives eventually formed their own party, they are better remembered as intellectuals and activists who wanted to reform politics. Such important political commentators as Herbert Croly (founder and editor of the *New Republic*), Henry Jones Ford, and politicians such as Woodrow Wilson, all urged important changes in the political system. This rather complex group of diverse people were united by the belief that the problems of democracy could be solved by more democracy. To do this, many Progressive reformers demanded significant changes in the party system. As a result, they significantly weakened party organizations and transformed the entire role the parties had served in governing.

The reforms struck at the very heart of the way parties operated. The first major reform, the secret ballot (also called the Australian ballot), actually predated much of the Progressive movement. Yet it was still an important change that reflected a broader attempt to curb party power. In the early years of the Republic, voting was done publicly and orally. This ideal harkened back to an older notion of democratic rule that demanded a public accounting of *both* citizens and rulers. In a republic, where citizens ruled, each individual should make his or her voice heard. In fact, citizenship was equated with an office that required a public display of opinion. In an era of strong parties, of course, this often resulted in an immense amount of peer pressure to vote a certain way. Even where printed ballots were used, it was often the case that party ballots were issued. In this case it was difficult, though not impossible, to avoid the straight party line. (Names could be crossed out, for instance. However, this was done publicly and added a burden to voting.) All of this made parties powerful social institutions that encouraged conformity and gave them a powerful tool in maintaining loyalty.

The Progressives urged the adoption of the secret ballot for just the reasons parties wanted to avoid them. Citizens, according to the Progressives, needed to think independently about politics, free from the pressures of group and organizational identity. The best candidate, and not the favored party, should garner our political support. This necessarily meant that it became easier for people to divide their votes between the different parties. Thus, the possibility of creating divided government increased with this reform. While this was not an automatic result, it was certainly possible, especially because the ideal of individual judgment took precedence over the need for party strength or government unity.

This first reform, while important, was not nearly as important as the rise of the primary system. Today, primaries are a well-integrated aspect of American political life. Again, this is largely a twentieth-century phenomenon. The Progressives wanted to weaken party organizations, and one way to do this was to remove the ability of such leaders ("bosses" in the lexicon of reformers) to control the selection process of candidates. In the nineteenth century, party conventions and caucuses were the primary vehicles for nominating candidates. However, today these methods are largely replaced by a primary system that allows all people who are part of the party to participate. Primaries were used immediately at the local and state level and, much later, became predominant at the national (or presidential) level. After 1968 the selection of the presidential nominee in either party was driven by the winning of delegates through primaries. This radically changed the relationship between candidates and citizens. Candidates, and later office holders, feel less beholden to party organizations. In some cases, they are actively hostile to the party organization that nominates them. Candidates, instead, are preoccupied with the attitudes of voters and especially the very limited electorate that votes in primaries. Only a fraction of the voters who show up in November cast ballots in primary elections, and highly motivated people, who do vote in primaries, often have political views that are more extreme than those of typical supporters of each party. The more typical voter—even the more typical partisan—is not necessarily represented by the primary results. A third party would not fundamentally alter this arrangement. The Reform Party's nomination process, which theoretically was open for all to participate in with its electronic methods, fell far short of creating a ground swell of involvement. The various efforts at opening up the process of selecting party nominees was supposed to increase the democratic involvement of citizens. Yet these reforms largely failed to achieve their stated goals.

The third great transformation undertaken in this century was civil service reform. From the 1880s onward, but accelerating in the next century, patronage yielded more and more to a professional, nonpartisan civil service. This is now true for virtually all but a handful of federal jobs. At the state and local level this took longer to develop, and it is still not true that a neutral, permanent civil service exists in all states and localities. This removed one final tool the parties had in generating loyalty.

Taken collectively, these reforms changed the two parties tremendously. Parties could no longer assume the normal straight ticket vote; they could no longer cajole and reward politicians with automatic nomination; finally, they no longer controlled the jobs—the ultimate plum to grant supporters. While none of these reforms were instant or universal, the overall result is clear: Parties became fundamentally different institutions from what they once were.

The question we must now address is: What have these reforms wrought? In large measure we can see that these changes in the party system bolstered the importance of money and media in American politics. In the name of more democracy we have relinquished the system over to the wealthy and to media sophisticates. This certainly has not made our political system more representative. In trying to make our institutions more responsive, we should reform the system to take the power of money and media into account and avoid looking for the creation of more choices. The use of the primaries forces another round of elections upon citizens and compels candidates to raise the money to manipulate the media and win such elections. We now increasingly talk about the "money" primary that occurs before the first actual vote is cast. Candidates raise money because they fear primary challenges and, at the presidential level, because they need vast amounts of cash to run in more than thirty state races to win nomination. Thus, candidates for president, such as Senator Phil Gramm, reminded audiences that serious contenders are those capable of raising huge amounts of cash, which, incidentally, are spent on the mass media. While Senator Gramm proves that money does not guarantee success, it is increasingly unlikely that a poorly funded candidate can win. This is the direct antithesis of the more interpersonal politics exhibited in the late nineteenth century and early twentieth century. This possibility was clearly seen by Henry Jones Ford, when the primary system was first created. Writing in 1909, Ford, a reformer, believed that the emerging system of rule would weaken parties and increase the power of money:

> The direct primary does not remove any of the conditions that have produced the [old, corrupt] system, but it intensifies their pressure by making politics still more confused, irresponsible, and costly. . . . The more elections there are, the larger becomes the class of professional politicians to be supported by the community.[30]

What Ford saw in the primary system is what we would also see with the creation of more political parties. The allure of more choices will cover the more dangerous probability that we are simply creating another layer of politicians who need our money. All of this would result in no greater representation of citizen interests.

The power of money and the evidence of corruption accounts for the present hostility toward American politics. President Washington's concerns are still timely in many ways. His worry that parties would open "the door to foreign influence" was prescient, given the embroilment of the Democratic National Committee (and the Republican National Committee) in controversy about Asian campaign contributions that followed the 1996 election. Instead of creating more parties, we would be better served by looking at serious campaign finance reform. The goal should not be more ideological choices, but more accountability to average citizens by the two parties we actually have. Part of Ross Perot's appeal in 1992 was based on this very concern about the way money corrupts our system. The ability of lobbyists and the wealthy to gain precious political access seriously undermines the confidence citizens have in their democracy. The irony of a multibillionaire championing such reforms should not let us lose sight of his very cogent criticisms. Furthermore, it makes more sense for the Reform Party to focus, like a single-issue interest group, on just this issue and not try its hand at becoming a third party.

Still, there are some good things about the progressive reforms and the system we have today. The present arrangement means that parties are porous organizations that are more open to being captured by reformers, activists, and those new to political life. We need only think about the recent attempts by the Christian Right to take control of Republican Party committees and influence the presidential primaries. Parties are often still criticized for being ruled by "bosses" and being closed off from the people. In reality the era of the bosses is long gone and parties represent whoever shows up to vote in the primary or organizes the meetings.

If the past thirty years of politics have taught us anything, it is that both political parties are just the sorts of institutions that can serve as avenues to new political activists. In 1964 the Republican Party was taken over by extreme conservatives whose champion was Barry Goldwater. The Democratic Party followed suit in 1972 with the nomination of the extremely liberal George McGovern. While many lament the choice of such candidates for their extremism and inability to win, more centrist candidates sometimes feel the same sense of possibility. When General Colin Powell ultimately revealed his affiliation with the Republican Party, he said that it was, partially, because one could only work effectively through the major parties. He, of course, wants to change the Republican Party, but the essential point is that he thinks that the Republican Party is a vehicle open to modification.

The fact is that politics have evolved as America has changed. Parties are

necessary in maintaining that fine balance between the desire for mass participation and the need for good government. The two parties served well in the
nineteenth century as a conduit between the people and the government. In
this century, both parties have tried to find new ways to fulfill that role. Although neither party has been fully successful, this does not mean that more
parties would solve the problem. We must keep in mind all of the many political goals we cherish. We need institutions that represent us in Washington,
that reflect ideological diversity and that make our government work with a
fair amount of effectiveness. The two parties historically accomplished these
many and varied tasks.

The alternative would be more parties that would most likely succeed in
one area very well (providing more ideological choices, for instance) while
diminishing government effectiveness (through increased gridlock). Representative democracy is a tricky thing to make work and the two parties helped
make it work for over two hundred years.

Conclusion

> They [the two parties] are absolutely necessary to hold the things thus
> disconnected and dispersed together and give some coherence to the ac-
> tion of political forces.
>
> *Woodrow Wilson*

The two great parties survive. Some argue that they survive only through the
"artificial" aid of unfair legal rules that preclude other parties from developing. If we only had more parties, we might have a better political system. This
is not the case. The answer to our political problems are not to be found in
the creation of more parties so that we might have the illusion of more choices;
rather, we should think about ways to improve the two parties we have today.
We must find ways that make parties accountable to citizens and not simply
responsive to the call of money. As we have seen, there are both reasons that
encourage a two-party system and reasons that make us thankful we only have
two parties.

First of all, America needs institutions that mediate between respecting diversity and aggregating political force sufficient for change. The two parties
do just that and they are capable of making the national government work.
The system of checks and balances, which Lowi objects to, is the defining
characteristic of our politics. If we still accept the basic nature of government,
then we need the two parties to impart a fair, but not excessive, amount of
efficiency to get things done. Furthermore, the political parties are the only
forces with enough power to overcome the natural state of gridlock that is the
hallmark of our politics. They create opportunities for leaders within Con-

gress, and the president outside of it, to find allies and work together for common goals.

America has successfully balanced the philosophical struggle between those who believe in individual liberty and civil order and those who champion social equality and the demands of justice. The belief in liberty and the claim of equality are central American beliefs—beliefs that often come into conflict. Although there is a great deal of ideological diversity in both parties, they in large measure serve to remind us of this deeper debate. More political parties would most likely divert our attention from this ongoing American argument. There is still something to be said for the existence of an identifiable, ideological difference between the Republican and Democratic Parties. At the end of the political day, these conflicting and competing principles provide a greater civic balance. While many may lament the lack of greater ideological choices, a key philosophical difference underlies both of these parties.

Along with these structural forces, there are cultural reasons why the two-party system is a positive good in our system. In a nation of great diversity the two-party system forces diverse people to unite and work together. It requires people to coalesce behind a slate of candidates when many of us would rather not—for ideological or personal reasons. Thus, political parties have served not only to unify government; they unify the nation as well. When James Madison talked about the existence of so many factions existing in the country, he thought this was a good thing; however, he also recognized that it would lead to great conflict. Two political parties help mitigate that conflict. They constrain the conflict by setting up two parties that unite a wide range of diverse people, all intent on capturing the national government. Alone, no one group could do that—but united they could.

The two parties foster lively conflict by encouraging disparate groups to come together and select a slate of candidates; then they foster a healthy consensus for the grander fight in the general election. Political parties teach people to work together for a common goal. An institution was created that molded together people of vastly different perspectives and goals. We need only think of the diversity of the New Deal coalition or the more recent amalgam of forces that make up the contemporary Republican Party to confirm this point.

To some, all of these reasons are frustrating: people must compromise on principles to join a winning party. However, this is the essence of democracy—compromise between people. Democracy requires people to talk to each other, to accept the possibility of defeat, and to respect their fellow citizens. While such things are possible with a third or fourth party, they become less and less likely. Democracy is about choice, but it is not synonymous with endless choices. Why should I agree to compromises within my party, when I can easily join others of like mind to form a third party or a fourth party?

Third parties encourage people to break away from the larger group in search of only akin people. Such "breaking away" would occur more and more frequently among the "team" of officeholders who make up the parties. This would create more gridlock and confusion among our leaders. However, that is only part of the story, because it would also foster bewilderment among voters in their increasingly desperate attempt to understand what is going on in Washington (and Trenton, and Annapolis, etc.). In a land as diverse and varied as America, this could be fatal. In a nation of so many different peoples and with so much individual freedom, the two-party system is an important institution that cements the bonds of political friendship so necessary for civil discourse. Democracy needs to be modified to work; we need to learn to accept defeat and to accept that others need us and that we need them. This is something all Americans must learn—citizens and their leaders. America's two great parties, at their best, teach this lesson by reminding us that we must work together and sacrifice a part of what we desire to make the entire project of American democracy work.

Major Third Parties or Third Candidates Since 1864

Year	Candidates	Party	Percent of Vote	Electoral Votes
1892	James Weaver	Populist	8.5	22
1912	Theodore Roosevelt	Bull-Moose	27.4	88
	Eugene V. Debs	Socialist	6.0	0
1924	Robert La Follette	Progressive	16.6	13
1948	Strom Thurmond	States' Rights	2.4	39
	Henry Wallace	Progressive	2.4	0
1968	George Wallace	American Independent	13.5	46
1980	John Anderson	Independent	6.6	0
1992	Ross Perot	Independent	18.9	0
1996	Ross Perot	Reform	8.6	0

Notes

1. See James Morone's insightful book *The Democratic Wish* (Basic Books: New York, 1990).

2. Susan Tolchin, *The Angry American* (Boulder, Colo.: Westview, 1996).

3. We should note that some recent scholarship indicates that parties are summoning no response—either positive or negative—from a great many citizens. This is possibly even worse; indifference can be more fatal to an institution than outright hostility.

4. Of course, as anyone who has ever voted notices, there are always numerous minor party candidates and many parties contesting for most offices. However, this essay deals with viable candidates and parties.

5. Due to the various and arcane laws of the different states, Perot's party is sometimes referred to as the Reform Party or as United We Stand. This is one more example of the federal principle at work.

6. William Riordon, *Plunkitt of Tammany Hall* (New York: E.P. Dutton, 1963), 13.

7. See A. James Reichley, *The Life of the Parties* (New York: Free Press, 1992).

8. Alexis de Tocqueville, *Democracy in America*, Vol. 1 (New York: Vintage Press, 1990), chap. 15, 263.

9. George Washington, "Farewell Address," *George Washington: Writings* (New York: Library of America, 1997), 970.

10. Thomas Jefferson, *The Portable Jefferson* (New York: Penguin Press, 1988), 435. Jefferson's inaugural remark "We have called by different names brethen of the same principle. We are all Republicans, we are all Federalists" might be read as a continued example of his hope to overcome the partisanship that he helped foster.

11. Federalist, Number 51.

12. Federalist, Number 51.

13. Quoted in Ross Baker's *House and Senate* (New York: Norton, 1989), 105.

14. This point is made clear in John Kingdon's *Agendas, Alternatives, and Public Policies* (New York: HarperCollins, 1995).

15. Federalist, Number 10.

16. This is the classic argument advanced by Maurice Duverger.

17. There is always concern about the possibility of the unfaithful elector. After all, electors are actual people with all the foibles that implies. However, there have been only a handful of faithless electors historically; although a multiparty system might encourage more such activity if no one party actually won the election.

18. Judith Best, *The Choice of the People: Debating the Electoral College* (Lanham, Md.: Rowman & Littlefield, 1996).

19. See Gerald Pomper, "From Confusion to Clarity: Issues and American Voters," in *Voters, Elections, and Parties* (New Brunswick, N.J.: Transaction Press, 1988).

20. Tocqueville, *Democracy in America*, Vol. 11, 115.

21. Robert Putnam, "Bowling Alone," *Journal of Democracy* 6:1 (January 1995): 65–78.

22. See Robert Bellah, *Habits of the Heart* (New York: Harper & Row, 1985).

23. Increasingly, television executives accept the fact that African Americans and white Americans watch different programs. For a superb accounting of the general

difficulties of whites and blacks living together, see Clarence Page's *Showing My Color* (New York: HarperCollins, 1996).

24. On this point, see Louis Hartz's provocative and still useful *The Liberal Tradition in America* (New York: Harcourt, Brace and Jovanovich, 1991). America's lack of a feudal past simplifies the ideological conflicts we have.

25. See Samuel Popkin, *The Reasoning Voter* (Chicago: University of Chicago Press, 1991).

26. Federalist, Number 10.

27. William L. Riordon, *Plunkitt of Tammany Hall*, p. 25.

28. See Mary K. Simkhovitch's wonderful essay "Friendship and Politics," in *Political Science Quarterly*, Vol. 17, No. 2 (June, 1902): 189–205.

29. Federalist, Number 16.

30. Henry Jones Ford, "The Direct Primary," *North American Review*, Vol. 190 (July, 1909): 4.

Select Bibliography

Aldrich, John. *Why Parties?* Chicago: University of Chicago Press, 1995.

Argersinger, Peter. *Structure, Process, and Party—Essays in American Political History.* Armonk, N.Y.: M. E. Sharpe, 1992.

Baker, Ross. *House and Senate.* New York: Norton, 1989.

Bellah, Robert, et al. *Habits of the Heart.* New York: Harper & Row, 1985.

Best, Judith. *The Choice of the People.* Lanham, Md.: Rowman & Littlefield, 1996.

Burke, Edmund. *Writing and Speeches of Edmund Burke.* Oxford: Oxford University Press, 1981.

Edsall, Thomas and Mary Edsall. *Chain Reaction.* New York: Norton, 1992.

———. *The New Politics of Inequality.* New York: Norton, 1984.

Epstein, Leon. *Political Parties in Western Democracies.* New Brunswick, N.J.: Transaction Press, 1979.

Flanigan, William and Nancy Zingale. *Political Behavior of the American Electorate.* Washington, D.C.: CQ Press, 1994.

Ford, Henry Jones. "The Direct Primary," *North American Review* 190, July, 1909.

Green, John and Daniel Shea. *The State of the Parties.* Lanham, Md.: Rowman & Littlefield, 1996.

Gross, Bertram M. *Friendly Fascism: The New Face of Power in America.* New York: M. Evans, 1980.

Hamilton, Alexander, James Madison and John Jay. *The Federalist Papers.* New York: New American Library, 1961.

Hartz, Louis. *The Liberal Tradition in America.* New York: Harcourt, Brace, Jovanovich, 1991.

Jefferson, Thomas. *The Portable Jefferson.* New York: Penguin Press, 1988.

Keith, Bruce, et al. *The Myth of the Independent Voter.* Berkeley: University of California Press, 1992.

Kingdon, John W. *Agendas, Alternatives, and Public Policy.* New York: HarperCollins, 1995.

Lowi, Theodore. *The End of the Republican Era.* Norman: University of Oklahoma Press, 1995.

———. "It Is Time for a Third Major Party in America." In *Controversial Issues in Presidential Selection,* ed. Gary L. Rose. Albany, N.Y.: State University of New York Press, 1994.

————. "The Time Is Ripe for the Creation of a Genuine Three-Party System," *The Chronicle of Higher Education.* 16 December 1992.

————. "The Party Crasher," *The New York Times Magazine.* 23 August 1992, 28, 33.

————. *The Personal Presidency.* Ithaca, N.Y.: Cornell University Press, 1985.

————. "Party, Policy, and Constitution in America." In *The American Party Systems: Stages of Political Development,* ed. William N. Chambers and Walter Dean Burnham. New York: Oxford University Press, 1975.

————. *The End of Liberalism.* New York: Norton, 1969.

Lubell, Samuel. *The Future of American Politics.* New York: Doubleday, 1952.

Maisel, L. Sandy. *The Parties Respond.* Boulder, Colo.: Westview Press, 1998.

Morone, James. *The Democratic Wish.* New York: Basic Books, 1990.

Page, Clarence. *Showing My Color.* New York: HarperCollins, 1996.

Polsby, Nelson, and Aaron Wildavsky. *Presidential Elections.* Chatham, N.J.: Chatham House, 1996.

Pomper, Gerald. *Passions and Interests.* Lawrence, Kansas: University Press of Kansas, 1992.

————. *Voters, Elections, and Parties.* New Brunswick, N.J.: Transaction Press, 1988.

————. *Elections in America.* New York: Dodd, Mead & Company, 1971.

Popkin, Samuel. *The Reasoning Voter.* Chicago: University of Chicago Press, 1991.

Putnam, Robert. "Bowling Alone," *Journal of Democracy* 6:1. January 1995.

Reichley, A. James. *The Life of the Parties.* New York: Free Press, 1992.

Riordon, William. *Plunkitt of Tammany Hall.* New York: E.P. Dutton, 1963.

Rosenstone, Steven, Roy Behr and Edward Lazarus. *Third Parties in America.* Princeton: Princeton University Press, 1996.

Schlesinger, Joseph. *Political Parties and the Winning of Office.* Ann Arbor: University of Michigan Press, 1994.

Silbey, Joel. *The American Political Nation, 1838–1893.* Stanford: Stanford University Press, 1991.

Simkhovitch, Mary. "Friendship and Politics," *Political Science Quarterly* 17, no. 2, July, 1902.

Tocqueville, Alexis de. *Democracy in America.* New York: Vintage, 1990.

Tolchin, Susan. *The Angry American.* Boulder, Colo.: Westview Press, 1996.

Walsh, Elsa. "Kennedy's Hidden Campaign," *The New Yorker Magazine.* 7 April 1997.

Ware, Alan. *Political Parties and Party Systems.* Oxford: Oxford University Press, 1996.

Washington, George. *George Washington: Writings.* New York: Library of America, 1997.

Wattenberg, Martin. *The Decline of American Political Parties.* Cambridge: Harvard University Press, 1996.

Wilson, James Q. *Political Organizations.* Princeton: Princeton University Press, 1995.

Wilson, Woodrow. *Constitutional Government in the United States.* New York: Columbia University Press, 1961.

Part Two

Readings

Editors' Introduction

Since the founding of the Republic, political parties have generated a great deal of commentary. Not surprisingly, many influential politicians and political thinkers have written specifically about this subject. The following documents highlight this ongoing debate about the proper role of parties in the American political system.

These documents fall into three categories. First, we include two articles from *The Federalist Papers*, written by James Madison. The essays included here offer a sophisticated defense of the Constitution at the time of its adoption. Part of that defense deals with the role of what Madison identifies as factions in this new government. When Madison refers to factions, he is most likely referring to what we classify as parties today. Madison argued that, although factions have their problems, they are an essential part of any political system dedicated to the preservation of individual freedom. Readers may judge for themselves whether Madison would approve of a two-party system or a multiparty system, given the arguments presented in these two essays.

The next three readings represents the thoughts on parties of three American presidents: George Washington, Thomas Jefferson, and Woodrow Wilson. In Washington's case, his *Farewell Address* included a spirited attack on the very idea of parties. To Washington they represented all that was dangerous and divisive in the world of politics. Just a few years later, Thomas Jefferson's first inaugural address indicates his acceptance of the reality of the two-party system—although, this acceptance fell far short of an endorsement of the permanence of such a system. Finally, by the beginning of the twentieth century, Woodrow Wilson told his audience that the Democratic party served to help the nation reach its most cherished goals. Parties had moved from being reviled to being the chosen instrument for national greatness.

These rather mixed messages about political parties are also reflected in the opinions of the Supreme Court. Throughout its history, the Court has been forced to deal with the ambiguous, yet central, role of the parties in American politics. Three recent cases illustrate the legal debates concerning parties.

First, in 1976, in *Elrod v. Burns*, the Court severely limited the ability of parties to fire government employees after the party had assumed power. Thus, patronage was legally limited. This trend in legal doctrine was extended in *Rutan v. Republican Party of Illinois* in 1989. Included, though, is an eloquent dissent, by Justice Antonin Scalia, that defends the role of patronage and the two-party system. Finally, most recently, in *Timmons v. Twin Cities Area New Party*, 1996, the Court upheld the right of the state of Minnesota to ban fusion tickets. Such methods allow a third party to nominate one of the candidates of major parties on its ballot. Thus, the third party hopes to attract some of the support from one of the major parties. The Court did not say that such activities are unconstitutional (the state of New York, for instance, allows it); however, states can proscribe such actions. Although the *Timmons* case was decided the way Lowi believed it would be, the Supreme Court may decide differently as new cases come forward.

1

James Madison,
The Federalist Papers, No. 10

Among the numerous advantages promised by a well-constructed Union, none deserves to be more accurately developed than its tendency to break and control the violence of faction. The friend of popular governments never finds himself so much alarmed for their character and fate as when he contemplates their propensity to this dangerous vice. He will not fail, therefore, to set a due value on any plan which, without violating the principles to which he is attached, provides a proper cure for it. The instability, injustice, and confusion introduced into the public councils have, in truth, been the mortal diseases under which popular governments have everywhere perished, as they continue to be the favorite and fruitful topics from which the adversaries to liberty derive their most specious declamations. The valuable improvements made by the American constitutions on the popular models, both ancient and modern, cannot certainly be too much admired; but it would be an unwarrantable partiality to contend that they have as effectually obviated the danger on this side, as was wished and expected. Complaints are everywhere heard from our most considerate and virtuous citizens, equally the friends of public and private faith and of public and personal liberty, that our governments are too unstable, that the public good is disregarded in the conflicts of rival parties, and that measures are too often decided, not according to the rules of justice and the rights of the minor party, but by the superior force of an interested and overbearing majority. However anxiously we may wish that these complaints had no foundation, the evidence of known facts will not permit us to deny that they are in some degree true. It will be found, indeed, on a candid review of our situation, that some of the distresses under which we labor have been erroneously charged on the operation of our governments; but it will be found, at the same time, that other causes will not alone account for many of our heaviest misfortunes; and, particularly, for that prevailing and increasing distrust of public engagements and alarm for private rights which are echoed from one end of the continent to the other. These must be chiefly, if not wholly, effects of the unsteadiness and injustice with which a factious spirit has tainted our public administration.

By a faction I understand a number of citizens, whether amounting to a majority or minority of the whole, who are united and actuated by some common impulse of passion, or of interest, adverse to the rights of other citizens, or to the permanent and aggregate interests of the community.

There are two methods of curing the mischiefs of faction: the one, by removing its causes; the other, by controlling its effects.

There are again two methods of removing the causes of faction: the one, by destroying the liberty which is essential to its existence; the other, by giving to every citizen the same opinions, the same passions, and the same interests.

It could never be more truly said than of the first remedy that it was worse than the disease. Liberty is to faction what air is to fire, an ailment without which it instantly expires. But it could not be a less folly to abolish liberty, which is essential to political life, because it nourishes faction than it would be to wish the annihilation of air, which is essential to animal life, because it imparts to fire its destructive agency.

The second expedient is as impracticable as the first would be unwise. As long as the reason of man continues fallible, and he is at liberty to exercise it, different opinions will be formed. As long as the connection subsists between his reason and his self-love, his opinions and his passions will have a reciprocal influence on each other; and the former will be objects to which the latter will attach themselves. . . . From the protection of different and unequal faculties of acquiring property, the possession of different degrees and kinds of property immediately results; and from the influence of these on the sentiments and views of the respective proprietors ensues a division of the society into different interests and parties.

The latent causes of faction are thus sown in the nature of man; and we see them everywhere brought into different degrees of activity, according to the different circumstances of civil society. A zeal for different opinions concerning religion, concerning government, and many other points, as well of speculation as of practice; an attachment to different leaders ambitiously contending for pre-eminence and power; or to persons of other descriptions whose fortunes have been interesting to the human passions, have, in turn, divided mankind into parties, inflamed them with mutual animosity, and rendered them much more disposed to vex and oppress each other than to co-operate for their common good. . . . But the most common and durable source of factions has been the verious and unequal distribution of property. Those who hold and those who are without property have ever formed distinct interests in society. Those who are creditors, and those who are debtors, fall under a like discrimination. A landed interest, a manufacturing interest, a mercantile interest, a moneyed interest, with many lesser interests, grow up of necessity in civilized nations, and divide them into different classes, actuated by different sentiments and views. The regulation of these various and interfering interests forms the principal task of modern legislation and involves the spirit of party and faction in the necessary and ordinary operations of government.

No man is allowed to be a judge in his own cause, because his interest would certainly bias his judgment, and, not improbably, corrupt his integrity. With equal, nay with greater reason, a body of men are unfit to be both judges and parties at the same time; yet what are many of the most important acts of legislation but so many judicial determinations, not indeed concerning the rights of single persons, but concerning the rights of large bodies of citizens? And what are the different classes of legislators but advocates and parties to the causes which they determine? Is a law proposed concerning private debts? It is a question to which the creditors are parties on one side and the debtors on the other. Justice ought to hold the balance between them. Yet the parties are, and must be, themselves the judges; and the most numerous party, or in other words, the most powerful faction must be expected to prevail. Shall domestic manufacturers be encouraged, and in what degree, by restrictions on foreign manufacturers? are questions which would be differently decided by the landed and the manufacturing classes, and probably by neither with a sole regard to justice and the public good. . . .

It is in vain to say that enlightened statesmen will be able to adjust these clashing interests and render them all subservient to the public good. Enlightened statesmen will not always be at the helm. Nor, in many cases, can such an adjustment be made at all without taking into view indirect and remote considerations, which will rarely prevail over the immediate interest which one party may find in disregarding the rights of another or the good of the whole.

The inference to which we are brought is that the *causes* of faction cannot be removed and that relief is only to be sought in the means of controlling its *effects*.

If a faction consists of less than a majority, relief is supplied by the republican principle, which enables the majority to defeat its sinister views by regular vote. It may clog the administration, it may convulse the society; but it will be unable to execute and mask its violence under the forms of the Constitution. When a majority is included in a faction, the form of popular government, on the other hand, enables it to sacrifice to its ruling passion or interest both the public good and the rights of other citizens. To secure the public good and private rights against the danger of such a faction, and at the same time to preserve the spirit and the form of popular government, is then the great object to which our inquiries are directed. Let me add that it is the great desideratum by which alone this form of government can be rescued from the opprobrium under which it has so long labored and be recommended to the esteem and adoption of mankind.

By what means is this object attainable? Evidently by one of two only. Either the existence of the same passion or interest in a majority at the same time must be prevented, or the majority, having such coexistent passion or interest, must be rendered, by their number and local situation, unable to concert and carry into effect schemes of oppression. If the impulse and the opportunity be suffered to coincide, we well know that neither moral nor religious motives can be relied on as an adequate control. They are not found to be such on the injustice and violence of individuals, and lose their efficacy in proportion to the number combined together, that is, in proportion as their efficacy becomes needful.

From this view of the subject it may be concluded that a pure democracy, by which I mean a society consisting of a small number of citizens, who assemble and administer the government in person, can admit of no cure for the mischiefs of faction. A common passion or interest will, in almost every case, be felt by a majority of the whole; a communication and concert results from the form of government itself; and there is nothing to check the inducements to sacrifice the weaker party or an obnoxious individual. Hence it is that such democracies have ever been spectacles of turbulence and contention; have ever been found incompatible with personal security or the rights of property; and have in general been as short in their lives as they have been violent in their deaths. . . .

A republic, by which I mean a government in which the scheme of representation takes place, opens a different prospect and promises the cure for which we are seeking. Let us examine the points in which it varies from pure democracy, and we shall comprehend both the nature of the cure and the efficacy which it must derive from the Union.

The two great points of difference between a democracy and a republic are: first, the delegation of the government, in the latter, to a small number of citizens elected by the rest; secondly, the greater number of citizens and greater sphere of country over which the latter may be extended.

The effect of the first difference is, on the one hand, to refine and enlarge the public views by passing them through the medium of a chosen body of citizens, whose wisdom may best discern the true interest of their country and whose patriotism and love of justice will be least likely to sacrifice it to temporary or partial considerations. Under such a regulation it may well happen that the public voice, pronounced by the representatives of the people, will be more consonant to the public good than if pronounced by the people themselves, convened for the purpose. On the other hand, the effect may be inverted. Men of factious tempers, of local prejudices, or of sinister designs, may, by intrigue, by corruption, or by other means, first obtain the suffrages, and then betray the interests of the people. The question resulting is, whether

small or extensive republics are most favorable to the election of proper guard-
ians of the public weal; and it is clearly decided in favor of the latter by two
obvious considerations.

In the first place it is to be remarked that however small the republic may
be the representatives must be raised to a certain number in order to guard
against the cabals of a few; and that however large it may be they must be
limited to a certain number in order to guard against the confusion of a multitude. Hence, the number of representatives in the two cases not being in proportion to that of the constituents, and being proportionally greatest in the
small republic, it follows that if the proportion of fit characters be not less in
the large than in the small republic, the former will present a greater option,
and consequently a greater probability of a fit choice.

In the next place, as each representative will be chosen by a greater number
of citizens in the large than in the small republic, it will be more difficult for
unworthy candidates to practise with success the vicious arts by which elections are too often carried; and the suffrages of the people being more free,
will be more likely to center on men who possess the most attractive merit
and the most diffusive and established characters.

It must be confessed that in this, as in most other cases, there is a mean, on
both sides of which inconveniencies will be found to lie. By enlarging too
much the number of electors, you render the representative too little ac-
quainted with all their local circumstances and lesser interests; as by reducing
it too much, you render him unduly attached to these, and too little fit to
comprehend and pursue great and national objects. The federal Constitution
forms a happy combination in this respect; the great and aggregate interests
being referred to the national, the local and particular to the State legislatures.

The other point of difference is the greater number of citizens and extent
of territory which may be brought within the compass of republican than of
democratic government; and it is this circumstance principally which renders
factious combinations less to be dreaded in the former than in the latter. The
smaller the society, the fewer probably will be the distinct parties and interests
composing it; the fewer the distinct parties and interests, the more frequently
will a majority be found of the same party; and the smaller the number of
individuals composing a majority, and the smaller the compass within which
they are placed, the more easily will they concert and execute their plans of
oppression. Extend the sphere and you take in a greater variety of parties and
interests; you make it less probable that a majority of the whole will have a
common motive to invade the rights of other citizens; or if such a common
motive exists, it will be more difficult for all who feel it to discover their own
strength and to act in unison with each other. . . .

The influence of factious leaders may kindle a flame within their particular
States but will be unable to spread a general conflagration through the other
States. A religious sect may degenerate into a political faction in a part of the

Confederacy; but the variety of sects dispersed over the entire face of it must secure the national councils against any danger from that source. A rage for paper money, for an abolition of debts, for an equal division of property, or for any other improper or wicked project, will be less apt to pervade the whole body of the Union than a particular member of it, in the same proportion as such a malady is more likely to taint a particular county or district than an entire State.

In the extent and proper structure of the Union, therefore, we behold a republican remedy for the diseases most incident to republican government. And according to the degree of pleasure and pride we feel in being republicans ought to be our zeal in cherishing the spirit and supporting the character of federalists.

2

James Madison,
The Federalist Papers, No. 51

. . . In order to lay a due foundation for that separate and distinct exercise of the different powers of government, which to a certain extent is admitted on all hands to be essential to the preservation of liberty, it is evident that each department should have a will of its own; and consequently should be so constituted that the members of each should have as little agency as possible in the appointment of the members of the others. Were this principle rigorously adhered to, it would require that all the appointments for the supreme executive, legislative, and judiciary magistracies should be drawn from the same fountain of authority, the people, through channels having no communication whatever with one another. Perhaps such a plan of constructing the several departments would be less difficult in practice than it may in contemplation appear. Some difficulties, however, and some additional expense would attend the execution of it. Some deviations, therefore, from the principle must be admitted. In the constitution of the judiciary department in particular, it might be inexpedient to insist rigorously on the principle: first, because peculiar qualifications being essential in the members, the primary consideration ought to be to select that mode of choice which best secures these qualifications; second, because the permanent tenure by which the appointments are held in that department must soon destroy all sense of dependence on the authority conferring them.

It is equally evident that the members of each department should be as little dependent as possible on those of the others for the emoluments annexed to their offices. Were the executive magistrate, or the judges, not independent of the legislature in this particular, their independence in every other would be merely nominal.

But the great security against a gradual concentration of the several powers in the same department consists in giving to those who administer each department the necessary constitutional means and personal motives to resist encroachments of the others. The provision for defense must in this, as in all other cases, be made commensurate to the danger of attack. Ambition must be made to counteract ambition. The interest of the man must be connected with the constitutional rights of the place. It may be a reflection on human nature that such devices should be necessary to control the abuses of government. But what is government itself but the greatest of all reflections on human nature? If men were angels, no government would be necessary. If angels were to govern men, neither external nor internal controls on government would be necessary. In framing a government which is to be administered by men over men, the great difficulty lies in this: you must first enable the government to control the governed; and in the next place oblige it to control itself. A dependence on the people is, no doubt, the primary control on the government; but experience has taught mankind the necessity of auxiliary precautions. . . .

But it is not possible to give to each department an equal power of self-defense. In republican government, the legislative authority necessarily predominates. The remedy for this inconveniency is to divide the legislature into different branches; and to render them, by different modes of election and different principles of action, as little connected with each other as the nature of their common functions and their common dependence on the society will admit. It may even be necessary to guard against dangerous encroachments by still further precautions. As the weight of the legislative authority requires that it should be thus divided, the weakness of the executive may require, on the other hand, that it should be fortified. An absolute negative on the legislature appears, at first view, to be the natural defense with which the executive magistrate should be armed. But perhaps it would be neither altogether safe nor alone sufficient. On ordinary occasions it might not be exerted with the requisite firmness, and on extraordinary occasions it might be perfidiously abused. May not this defect of an absolute negative be supplied by some qualified connection between this weaker department and the weaker branch of the stronger department, by which the latter may be led to support the constitutional rights of the former, without being too much detached from the rights of its own department? . . . There are, moreover, two considerations particularly applicable to the federal system of America, which place that system in a very interesting point of view.

First. In a single republic, all the power surrendered by the people is submitted to the administration of a single government; and the usurpations are guarded against by a division of the government into distinct and separate departments. In the compound republic of America, the power surrendered by the people is first divided between two distinct governments, and then the portion allotted to each subdivided among distinct and separate departments. Hence a double security arises to the rights of the people. The different governments will control each other, at the same time that each will be controlled by itself.

Second. It is of great importance in a republic not only to guard the society against the oppression of its rulers, but to guard one part of the society against the injustice of the other part. Different interests necessarily exist in different classes of citizens. If a majority be united by a common interest, the rights of the minority will be insecure. There are but two methods of providing against this evil: the one by creating a will in the community independent of the majority—that is, of the society itself; the other, by comprehending in the society so many separate descriptions of citizens as will render an unjust combination of a majority of the whole very improbable, if not impracticable. The first method prevails in all governments possessing an hereditary or self-appointed authority. This, at best, is but a precarious security; because a power independent of the society may as well espouse the unjust views of the major as the rightful interests of the minor party, and may possibly be turned against both parties. The second method will be exemplified in the federal republic of the United States. Whilst all authority in it will be derived from and dependent on the society, the society itself will be broken into so many parts, interests and classes of citizens, that the rights of individuals, or of the minority, will be in little danger from interested combinations of the majority. In a free government the security for civil rights must be the same as that for religious rights. It consists in the one case in the multiplicity of interests, and in the other in the multiplicity of sects. The degree of security in both cases will depend on the number of interests and sects; and this may be presumed to depend on the extent of country and number of people comprehended under the same government. This view of the subject must particularly recommend a proper federal system to all the sincere and considerate friends of republican government, since it shows that in exact proportion as the territory of the Union may be formed into more circumscribed Confederacies, or States, oppressive combinations of a majority will be facilitated; the best security, under the republican forms, for the rights of every class of citizen, will be diminished; and consequently the stability and independence of some member of the government, the only other security, must be proportionally increased. Justice is the end of government. It is the end of civil society. It ever has been and ever will be pursued until it be obtained, or until liberty be lost in the pursuit. . . .

In the extended republic of the United States, and among the great variety of interests, parties, and sects which it embraces, a coalition of a majority of the whole society could seldom take place on any other principles than those of justice and the general good; whilst there being thus less danger to a minor from the will of a majority party, there must be less pretext, also, to provide for the security of the former, by introducing into the government a will not dependent on the latter, or, in other words, a will independent of the society itself. It is no less certain than it is important, notwithstanding the contrary opinions which have been entertained, that the larger the society, provided it lie within a practicable sphere, the more duly capable it will be of self-government. And happily for the *republican cause,* the practicable sphere may be carried to a very great extent by a judicious modification and mixture of the *federal principle.*

3

George Washington, Farewell Address

. . . The Unity of Government which constitutes you one people is also now dear to you. It is justly so; for it is a main Pillar in the Edifice of your real independence, the support of your tranquility at home; your peace abroad; of your safety; of your prosperity; of that very Liberty which you so highly prize. But as it is easy to foresee, that from different causes and from different quarters, much pains will be taken, many artifices employed, to weaken in your minds the conviction of this truth; as this is the point in your political fortress against which the batteries of internal and external enemies will be most constantly and actively (though often covertly and insidiously) directed, it is of infinite moment, that you should properly estimate the immense value of your national Union to your collective and individual happiness; that you should cherish a cordial, habitual and immoveable attachment to it; accustoming yourselves to think and speak of it as of the Palladium of your political safety and prosperity; watching for its preservation with jealous anxiety; discountenancing whatever may suggest even a suspicion that it can in any event be abandoned, and indignantly frowning upon the first dawning of every attempt to alienate any portion of our Country from the rest, or to enfeeble the sacred ties which now link together the various parts. . . .

While then every part of our country thus feels an immediate and particular Interest in Union, all the parts combined cannot fail to find in the united mass of means and efforts greater strength, greater resources, proportionably greater security from external danger, a less frequent interruption of their Peace by foreign Nations; and, what is of inestimable value! they must derive from Union an exemption from those broils and Wars between themselves, which so frequently afflict neighbouring countries, not tied together by the same government; which their own rivalships alone would be sufficient to produce, but which opposite foreign alliances, attachments and intriegues would stimulate and imbitter. Hence likewise they will avoid the necessity of those overgrown Military establishments, which under any form of Government are inauspicious to liberty, and which are to be regarded as particularly

91

hostile to Republican Liberty: In this sense it is, that your Union ought to be considered as a main prop of your liberty, and that the love of the one ought to endear to you the preservation of the other.

In contemplating the causes wch. may disturb our Union, it occurs as matter of serious concern, that any ground should have been furnished for characterizing parties by *Geographical* discriminations: *Northern* and *Southern*; *Atlantic* and *Western*; whence designing men may endeavour to excite a belief that there is a real difference of local interests and views. One of the expedients of Party to acquire influence, within particular districts, is to misrepresent the opinions and aims of other Districts. You cannot shield yourselves too much against the jealousies and heart burnings which spring from these misrepresentations. They tend to render Alien to each other those who ought to be bound together by fraternal affection. . . .

All obstructions to the execution of the Laws, all combinations and Associations, under whatever plausible character, with the real design to direct, controul counteract, or awe the regular deliberation and action of the Constituted authorities are distructive of this fundamental principle and of fatal tendency. They serve to organize faction, to give it an artificial and extraordinary force; to put in the place of the delegated will of the Nation, the will of a party; often a small but artful and enterprizing minority of the Community; and, according to the alternate triumphs of different parties, to make the public administration the Mirror of the ill concerted and incongruous projects of faction, rather than the organ of consistent and wholesome plans digested by common councils and modefied by mutual interests. However combinations or Associations of the above description may now and then answer popular ends, they are likely, in the course of time and things, to become potent engines, by which cunning, ambitious and unprincipled men will be enabled to subvert the Power of the People, and to usurp for themselves the reins of Government; destroying afterwards the very engines which have lifted them to unjust dominion. . . .

I have already intimated to you the danger of Parties in the State, with particular reference to the founding of them on Geographical discriminations. Let me now take a more comprehensive view, and warn you in the most solemn manner against the baneful effects of the Spirit of Party, generally.

This spirit, unfortunately, is inseperable from our nature, having its root in the strongest passions of the human Mind. It exists under different shapes in all Governments, more or less stifled, controuled, or repressed; but, in those of the popular form it is seen in its greatest rankness and is truly their worst enemy.

The alternate domination of one faction over another, sharpened by the spirit of revenge natural to party dissension, which in different ages and countries has perpetrated the most horrid enormities, is itself a frightful despotism. But this leads at length to a more formal and permanent despotism. The disorders and miseries, which result, gradually incline the minds of men to seek security and repose in the absolute power of an Individual: and sooner or later the chief of some prevailing faction more able or more fortunate than his competitors, turns this disposition to the purposes of his own elevation, on the ruins of Public Liberty.

Without looking forward to an extremity of this kind (which nevertheless ought not to be entirely out of sight) the common and continual mischiefs of the spirit of Party are sufficient to make it the interest and the duty of a wise People to discourage and restrain it.

It serves always to distract the Public Councils and enfeeble the Public administration. It agitates the Community with ill founded jealousies and false alarms, kindles the animosity of one part against another, foments occasionally riot and insurrection. It opens the door to foreign influence and corruption, which find a facilitated access to the government itself through the channels of party passions. Thus the policy and the will of one country, are subjected to the policy and will of another.

There is an opinion that parties in free countries are useful checks upon the Administration of the Government and serve to keep alive the spirit of Liberty. This within certain limits is probably true, and in Governments of a Monarchical cast Patriotism may look with endulgence, if not with favour, upon the spirit of party. But in those of the popular character, in Governments purely elective, it is a spirit not to be encouraged. From their natural tendency, it is certain there will always be enough of that spirit for every salutary purpose. And there being constant danger of excess, the effort ought to be, by force of public opinion, to mitigate and assuage it. A fire not to be quenched; it demands a uniform vigilance to prevent its bursting into a flame, lest instead of warming it should consume.

4

Thomas Jefferson, First Inaugural Address

. . . During the contest of opinion through which we have passed the animation of discussions and of exertions has sometimes worn an aspect which might impose on strangers unused to think freely and to speak and to write what they think; but this being now decided by the voice of the nation, announced according to the rules of the Constitution, all will, of course, arrange themselves under the will of the law, and unite in common efforts for the common good. All, too, will bear in mind this sacred principle, that though the will of the majority is in all cases to prevail, that will to be rightful must be reasonable; that the minority possesses their equal rights, which equal law must protect, and to violate would be oppression. Let us, then, fellow-citizens, unite with one heart and one mind. Let us restore to social intercourse that harmony and affection without which liberty and even life itself are but dreary things. And let us reflect that, having banished from our land that religious intolerance under which mankind so long bled and suffered, we have yet gained little if we countenance a political intolerance as despotic, as wicked, and capable of as bitter and bloody persecutions. During the throes and convulsions of the ancient world, during the agonizing spasms of infuriated man, seeking through blood and slaughter his long-lost liberty, it was not wonderful that the agitation of the billows should reach even this distant and peaceful shore; that this should be more felt and eared by some and less by others, and should divide opinions as to measures of safety. But every difference of opinion is not a difference of principle. We have called by different names brethren of the same principle. We are all Republicans, we are all Federalists. If there be any among us who would wish to dissolve this Union or to change its republican form, let them stand undisturbed as monuments of the safety with which error of opinion may be tolerated where reason is left free to combat it. I know, indeed, that some honest men fear that a republican government can not be strong, that this Government is not strong enough; but would the honest patriot, in the full tide of successful experiment, abandon a government which has so far kept us free and firm on the theoretic and visionary fear that this Government, the world's best hope, may by possibility want energy to preserve itself? I trust not. I believe this, on the contrary, the strongest Government on earth. I believe it the only one where every man, at the call of the law, would fly to the standard of the law, and would meet invasions of the public order as his own personal concern. Sometimes it is said that man can not be trusted with the government of himself. Can he, then, be trusted with the government of others? Or have we found angels in the forms of kings to govern him? Let history answer this question.

Let us, then, with courage and confidence pursue our own Federal and Republican principles, our attachment to union and representative government. . . .

5

Woodrow Wilson, Inaugural Address

There has been a change of government. It began two years ago, when the House of Representatives became Democratic by a decisive majority. It has now been completed. The Senate about to assemble will also be Democratic. The offices of President and Vice-President have been put into the hands of Democrats. What does the change mean? That is the question that is upper-most in our minds to-day. That is the question I am going to try to answer, in order, if I may, to interpret the occasion.

It means much more than the mere success of a party. The success of a party means little except when the Nation is using that party for a large and definite purpose. No one can mistake the purpose for which the Nation now seeks to use the Democratic Party. It seeks to use it to interpret a change in its own plans and point of view. Some old things with which we had grown familiar, and which had begun to creep into the very habit of our thought and of our lives, have altered their aspect as we have latterly looked critically upon them, with fresh, awakened eyes; have dropped their disguises and shown themselves alien and sinister. Some new things, as we look frankly upon them, willing to comprehend their real character, have come to assume the aspect of things long believed in and familiar, stuff of our own convictions. We have been refreshed by a new insight into our own life. . . .

We have built up, moreover, a great system of government, which has stood through a long age as in many respects a model for those who seek to set liberty upon foundations that will endure against fortuitous change, against storm and accident. Our life contains every great thing, and contains it in rich abundance.

But the evil has come with the good, and much fine gold has been corroded. With riches has come inexcusable waste. We have squandered a great part of what we might have used, and have not stopped to conserve the exceeding bounty of nature, without which our genius for enterprise would have been worthless and impotent, scorning to be careful, shamefully prodigal as well as admirably efficient. We have been proud of our industrial achievements, but we have not hitherto stopped thoughtfully enough to count the human cost, the cost of lives snuffed out, of energies overtaxed and broken, the fearful physical and spiritual cost to the men and women and children upon whom the dead weight and burden of it all has fallen pitilessly the years through. The groans and agony of it all had not yet reached our ears, the solemn, moving undertone of our life, coming up out of the mines and factories, and out of every home where the struggle had its intimate and familiar seat. With the great Government went many deep secret things which we too long delayed to look into and scrutinize with candid, fearless eyes. The great Government we loved has too often been made use of for private and selfish purposes, and those who used it had forgotten the people.

At last a vision has been vouchsafed us of our life as a whole. We see the bad with the good, the debased and decadent with the sound and vital. With this vision we approach new affairs. Our duty is to cleanse, to reconsider, to restore, to correct the evil without impairing the good, to purify and humanize every process of our common life without weakening or sentimentalizing it. There has been something crude and heartless and unfeeling in our haste to succeed and be great. Our thought has been "Let every man look out for himself, let every generation look out for itself," while we reared giant machinery which made it impossible that any but those who stood at the levers of control should have a chance to look out for themselves. We had not forgotten our morals. We remembered well enough that we had set up a policy which was meant to serve the humblest as well as the most powerful, with an eye single to the standards of justice and fair play, and remembered it with pride. But we were very heedless and in a hurry to be great.

We have come now to the sober second thought. The scales of heedlessness have fallen from our eyes. We have made up our minds to square every process of our national life again with the standard we so proudly set up at the beginning and have always carried at our hearts. Our work is a work of restoration.

. . . This is the high enterprise of the new day: To lift everything that concerns our life as a Nation to the light that shines from the hearthfire of every man's conscience and vision of the right. It is inconceivable that we should do this as partisans; it is inconceivable we should do it in ignorance of the facts as they are or in blind haste. We shall restore, not destroy. We shall deal with our economic system as it is and as it may be modified, not as it might be if we had a clean sheet of paper to write upon; and step by step we shall make it what it should be, in the spirit of those who question their own wisdom and seek counsel and knowledge, not shallow self-satisfaction or the excitement of excursions whither they can not tell. Justice, and only justice, shall always be our motto. . . .

This is not a day of triumph; it is a day of dedication. Here muster, not the forces of party, but the forces of humanity. Men's hearts wait upon us; men's lives hang in the balance; men's hopes call upon us to say what we will do. Who shall live up to the great trust? Who dares fail to try? I summon all honest men, all patriotic, all forward-looking men, to my side. God helping me, I will not fail them, if they will but counsel and sustain me!

6

Elrod v. Burns

... The cost of the practice of patronage is the restraint it places on freedoms of belief and association. In order to maintain their jobs, respondents were required to pledge their political allegiance to the Democratic Party, work for the election of other candidates of the Democratic Party, contribute a portion of their wages to the Party, or obtain the sponsorship of a member of the Party, usually at the price of one of the first three alternatives. Regardless of the incumbent party's identity, Democratic or otherwise, the consequences for association and belief are the same. An individual who is a member of the out-party maintains affiliation with his own party at the risk of losing his job. He works for the election of his party's candidates and espouses its policies at the same risk. . . . Since the average public employee is hardly in the financial position to support his party and another, or to lend his time to two parties, the individual's ability to act according to his beliefs and to associate with others of his political persuasion is constrained, and support for his party is diminished.

It is not only belief and association which are restricted where political patronage is the practice. The free functioning of the electoral process also suffers. Conditioning public employment on partisan support prevents support of competing political interests. Existing employees are deterred from such support, as well as the multitude seeking jobs. . . . Patronage thus tips the electoral process in favor of the incumbent party, and where the practice's scope is substantial relative to the size of the electorate, the impact on the process can be significant.

Preservation of the democratic process is certainly an interest protection of which may in some instances justify limitations on First Amendment freedoms. But however important preservation of the two-party system or any system involving a fixed number of parties may or may not be, *Williams* v. *Rhodes, supra,* at 32, we are not persuaded that the elimination of patronage practice or, as is specifically involved here, the interdiction of patronage dismissals, will bring about the demise of party politics. Political parties existed in the absence of active patronage practice prior to the administration of Andrew Jackson, and they have survived substantial reduction in their patronage power through the establishment of merit systems.[1] . . .

---

1. Sorauf, The Silent Revolution in Patronage, 20 Pub. Admin. Rev. 28, 32–33 (1960); Sorauf, Patronage and Party, 3 Midwest J. Pol. Sci. 115, 118–120 (1959).

7

Rutan v. Republican Party of Illinois

. . . Today the Court establishes the constitutional principle that party membership is not a permissible factor in the dispensation of government jobs, except
those jobs for the performance of which party affiliation is an "appropriate
requirement." *Ante,* at 64. It is hard to say precisely (or even generally) what
that exception means, but if there is any category of jobs for whose performance party affiliation is not an appropriate requirement, it is the job of being
a judge, where partisanship is not only unneeded but positively undesirable.
It is, however, rare that a federal administration of one party will appoint a
judge from another party. And it has always been rare. See *Marbury* v. *Madison,* 1 Cranch 137 (1803). Thus, the new principle that the Court today an-
nounces will be enforced by a corps of judges (the Members of this Court
included) who overwhelmingly owe their office to its violation. Something
must be wrong here, and I suggest it is the Court.

The merit principle for government employment is probably the most favored in modern America, having been widely adopted by civil service legislation at both the state and federal levels. But there is another point of view,
described in characteristically Jacksonian fashion by an eminent practitioner
of the patronage system, George Washington Plunkitt of Tammany Hall:

> "I ain't up on sillygisms, but I can give you some arguments that nobody can
> answer.
> "First, this great and glorious country was built up by political parties; second,
> parties can't hold together if their workers don't get offices when they win; third,
> if the parties go to pieces, the government they built up must go to pieces, too;
> fourth, then there'll be hell to pay." W. Riordon, Plunkitt of Tammany Hall 13
> (1963).

It may well be that the Good Government Leagues of America were right, and
that Plunkitt, James Michael Curley, and their ilk were wrong; but that is
not entirely certain. As the merit principle has been extended and its effects

increasingly felt; as the Boss Tweeds, the Tammany Halls, the Pendergast Machines, the Byrd Machines, and the Daley Machines have faded into history; we find that political leaders at all levels increasingly complain of the helplessness of elected government, unprotected by "party discipline," before the demands of small and cohesive interest groups.

The choice between patronage and the merit principle—or, to be more realistic about it, the choice between the desirable mix of merit and patronage principles in widely varying federal, state, and local political contexts—is not so clear that I would be prepared, as an original matter, to chisel a single, inflexible prescription into the Constitution. . . . Today the Court makes its constitutional civil service reform absolute, extending to all decisions regarding government employment. Because the First Amendment has never been thought to require this disposition, which may well have disastrous consequences for our political system, I dissent. . . .

. . . The Court holds that the governmental benefits of patronage cannot reasonably be thought to outweigh its "coercive" effects (even the lesser "coercive" effects of patronage hiring as opposed to patronage firing) not merely in 1990 in the State of Illinois, but at any time in any of the numerous political subdivisions of this vast country. It seems to me that that categorical pronouncement reflects a naive vision of politics and an inadequate appreciation of the systemic effects of patronage in promoting political stability and facilitating the social and political integration of previously powerless groups.

The whole point of my dissent is that the desirability of patronage is a policy question to be decided by the people's representatives; I do not mean, therefore, to endorse that system. But in order to demonstrate that a legislature could reasonably determine that its benefits outweigh its "coercive" effects, I must describe those benefits as the proponents of patronage see them: As Justice Powell discussed at length in his *Elrod* dissent, patronage stabilizes political parties and prevents excessive political fragmentation—both of which are results in which States have a strong governmental interest. Party strength requires the efforts of the rank and file, especially in "the dull periods between elections," to perform such tasks as organizing precincts, registering new voters, and providing constituent services. . . . Even the most enthusiastic supporter of a party's program will shrink before such drudgery, and it is folly to think that ideological conviction alone will motivate sufficient numbers to keep the party going through the off years. "For the most part, as every political knows, the hope of some reward generates a major portion of the local political activity supporting parties." . . .

. . . Increased reliance on money-intensive campaign techniques tends to entrench those in power much more effectively than patronage—but without the attendant benefit of strengthening the party system. A challenger can more easily obtain the support of party workers (who can expect to be rewarded even if the candidate loses—if not this year, then the next) than the financial support of political action committees (which will generally support incumbents, who are likely to prevail).

It is self-evident that eliminating patronage will significantly undermine party discipline; and that as party discipline wanes, so will the strength of the two-party system. But, says the Court, "[p]olitical parties have already survived the substantial decline in patronage employment practices in this century." *Ante,* at 74. This is almost verbatim what was said in *Elrod,* see 427 U. S., at 369. Fourteen years later it seems much less convincing. Indeed, now that we have witnessed, in 18 of the last 22 years, an Executive Branch of the Federal Government under the control of one party while the Congress is entirely or (for two years) partially within the control of the other party; now that we have undergone the most recent federal election, in which 98% of the incumbents, of whatever party, were returned to office; and now that we have seen elected officials changing their political affiliation with unprecedented readiness. . . . Parties have assuredly survived—but as what? As the forges upon which many of the essential compromises of American political life are hammered out? Or merely as convenient vehicles for the conducting of national Presidential elections?

The patronage system does not, of course, merely foster political parties in general; it fosters the two-party system in particular. When getting a job, as opposed to effectuating a particular substantive policy, is an available incentive for party workers, those attracted by that incentive are likely to work for the party that has the best chance of displacing the "ins," rather than for some splinter group that has a more attractive political philosophy but little hope of success. Not only is a two-party system more likely to emerge, but the differences between those parties are more likely to be moderated, as each has a relatively greater interest in appealing to a majority of the electorate and a relatively lesser interest in furthering philosophies or programs that are far from the mainstream. The stabilizing effects of such a system are obvious. . . .

Equally apparent is the relatively destabilizing nature of a system in which candidates cannot rely upon patronage-based party loyalty for their campaign support, but must attract workers and raise funds by appealing to various interest groups. . . . There is little doubt that our decisions in *Elrod* and *Branti,* by contributing to the decline of party strength, have also contributed to the growth of interest-group politics in the last decade. . . . Our decision today will greatly accelerate the trend. It is not only campaigns that are affected, of course, but the subsequent behavior of politicians once they are in power. The replacement of a system firmly in party discipline with one in which each officeholder comes to his own accommodation with competing interest groups produces "a dispersion of political influence that may inhibit a political party from enacting its programs into law." . . .

Patronage, moreover, has been a powerful means of achieving the social and political integration of excluded groups. . . . By supporting and ultimately dominating a particular party "machine," racial and ethnic minorities have—on the basis of their politics rather than their race or ethnicity—acquired the patronage awards the machine had power to confer. No one disputes the historical accuracy of this observation, and there is no reason to think that patronage can no longer serve that function. The abolition of patronage, however, prevents groups that have only recently obtained political power, especially blacks, from following this path to economic and social advancement. . . .

While the patronage system has the benefits argued for above, it also has undoubted disadvantages. It facilitates financial corruption, such as salary kickbacks and partisan political activity on government-paid time. It reduces the efficiency of government, because it creates incentives to hire more and less qualified workers and because highly qualified workers are reluctant to accept jobs that may only last until the next election. And, of course, it applies some greater or lesser inducement for individuals to join and work for the party in power.

To hear the Court tell it, this last is the greatest evil. That is not my view, and it has not historically been the view of the American people. Corruption and inefficiency, rather than abridgment of liberty, have been the major criticisms leading to enactment of the civil service laws—for the very good reason that the patronage system does not have as harsh an effect upon conscience, expression, and association as the Court suggests. As described above, it is the nature of the pragmatic, patronage-based, two-party system to build alliances and to suppress rather than foster ideological tests for participation in the division of political "spoils." What the patronage system ordinarily demands of the party worker is loyalty to, and activity on behalf of, the organization itself rather than a set of political beliefs. He is generally free to urge *within the organization* the adoption of any political position; but if that position is rejected he must vote and work for the party nonetheless. . . . It is undeniable, of course, that the patronage system entails some constraint upon the expression of views, particularly at the partisan-election stage, and considerable constraint upon the employee's right to associate with the other party. It greatly exaggerates these, however, to describe them as a general " 'coercion of belief.' " . . .

. . . The choice in question, I emphasize, is not just between patronage and a merit-based civil service, but rather among various combinations of the two that may suit different political units and different eras: permitting patronage hiring, for example, but prohibiting patronage dismissal; permitting patronage in most municipal agencies but prohibiting it in the police department; or permitting it in the mayor's office but prohibiting it everywhere else. I find it impossible to say that, always and everywhere, all of these choices fail our "balancing" test. . . .

8

Timmons v. Twin Cities Area New Party

Justice Stevens, with whom Justice Ginsburg joins, and with whom Justice Souter joins as to Parts I and II, dissenting.

In Minnesota, the Twin Cities Area New Party (Party), is a recognized minor political party entitled by state law to have the names of its candidates for public office appear on the state ballots. In April, 1994, Andy Dawkins was qualified to be a candidate for election to the Minnesota Legislature as the representative of House District 65A. With Dawkins's consent, the Party nominated him as its candidate for that office. In my opinion the Party and its members had a constitutional right to have their candidate's name appear on the ballot despite the fact that he was also the nominee of another party.

The Court's conclusion that the Minnesota statute prohibiting multiple-party candidacies is constitutional rests on three dubious premises: (1) that the statute imposes only a minor burden on the Party's right to choose and to support the candidate of its choice; (2) that the statute significantly serves the State's asserted interests in avoiding ballot manipulation and factionalism; and (3) that, in any event, the interest in preserving the two-party system justifies the imposition of the burden at issue in this case. I disagree with each of these premises. . . .

. . . In most States, perhaps in all, there are two and only two major political parties. It is not surprising, therefore, that most States have enacted election laws that impose burdens on the development and growth of third parties. The law at issue in this case is undeniably such a law. The fact that the law was both intended to disadvantage minor parties and has had that effect is a matter that should weigh against, rather than in favor of, its constitutionality.[1]

---

1. Indeed, "[a] burden that falls unequally on new or small political parties or on independent candidates impinges, by its very nature, on associational choices protected by the First Amendment." *Anderson* v. *Celebrezze,* 460 U. S. 780, 793–794, (1983). I do not think it is irrelevant that when antifusion laws were passed by States all over the Nation in the latter part of the 1800's, these laws, characterized by the majority as "reforms" *ante,* at 4, were passed by "the parties in power in state legislatures . . . to

Our jurisprudence in this area reflects a certain tension: on the one hand, we have been clear that political stability is an important state interest and that incidental burdens on the formation of minor parties are reasonable to protect that interest, see *Storer,* 415 U. S., at 736; on the other, we have struck down state elections laws specifically because they give "the two old, established parties a decided advantage over any new parties struggling for existence." . . .

Nothing in the Constitution prohibits the States from maintaining single-member districts with winner-take-all voting arrangements. And these elements of an election system do make it significantly more difficult for third parties to thrive. But these laws are different in two respects from the fusion bans at issue here. First, the method by which they hamper third-party development is not one that impinges on the associational rights of those third parties; minor parties remain free to nominate candidates of their choice, and to rally support for those candidates. The small parties' relatively limited likelihood of ultimate success on election day does not deprive them of the right to try. Second, the establishment of single-member districts correlates directly with the States' interests in political stability. Systems of proportional representation, for example, may tend toward factionalism and fragile coalitions that diminish legislative effectiveness. In the context of fusion candidacies, the risks to political stability are extremely attenuated. Of course, the reason minor parties so ardently support fusion politics is because it allows the parties to build up a greater base of support, as potential minor party members realize that a vote for the smaller party candidate is not necessarily a "wasted" vote. Eventually, a minor party might gather sufficient strength that—were its members so inclined—it could successfully run a candidate not endorsed by any major party, and legislative coalition-building will be made more difficult by the presence of third party legislators. But the risks to political stability in that scenario are speculative at best.[2]

In some respects, the fusion candidacy is the best marriage of the virtues

---

squelch the threat posed by the opposition's combined voting force." *McKenna,* 73 F. 3d, at 198. See Argersinger, "A Place on the Ballot": Fusion Politics and Antifusion Laws, 85 Am. Hist. Rev. 287, 302–306 (1980). Although the State is not required now to justify its laws with exclusive reference to the original purpose behind their passage, *Bolger* v. *Youngs Drug Products Corp.,* 463 U. S. 60, 70–71 (1983), this history does provide some indication of the kind of burden the States themselves believed they were imposing on the smaller parties' effective association.

2. In fact, Minnesota's expressed concern that fusion candidacies would stifle political diversity because minor parties would not put additional names on the ballot seems directly contradictory to the majority's imposed interest in the stable two-party system. The tension between the Court's rationale for its decision and the State's actually articulated interests is one of the reasons I do not believe the Court can legitimately consider interests not relied on by the State, especially in a context where the burden imposed and the interest justifying it must have some relationship.

of the minor party challenge to entrenched viewpoints[3] and the political stability that the two-party system provides. The fusion candidacy does not threaten to divide the legislature and create significant risks of factionalism, which is the principal risk proponents of the two-party system point to. But it does provide a means by which voters with viewpoints not adequately represented by the platforms of the two major parties can indicate to a particular candidate that—in addition to his support for the major party views—he should be responsive to the views of the minor party whose support for him was demonstrated where political parties demonstrate support—on the ballot.

The strength of the two-party system—and of each of its major components—is the product of the power of the ideas, the traditions, the candidates, and the voters that constitute the parties.[4] It demeans the strength of the two-party system to assume that the major parties need to rely on laws that discriminate against independent voters and minor parties in order to preserve their positions of power.[5] Indeed, it is a central theme of our jurisprudence that the entire electorate, which necessarily includes the members of the major parties, will benefit from robust competition in ideas and governmental policies that " 'is at the core of our electoral process and of the First Amendment freedoms.' " . . .

In my opinion legislation that would otherwise be unconstitutional because it burdens First Amendment interests and discriminates against minor political parties cannot survive simply because it benefits the two major parties. Accordingly, I respectfully dissent.

---

3. "[A]s an outlet for frustration, often as a creative force and a sort of conscience, as an ideological governor to keep major parties from speeding off into an abyss of mindlessness, and even just as a technique for strengthening a group's bargaining position for the future, the minor party would have to be invented if it did not come into existence regularly enough." A. Bickel, Reform and Continuity 80 (1971); see also S. Rosenstone, R. Behr, & E. Lazarus, Third Parties in America: Citizen Response to Major Party Failure 4–9 (1984).

4. The Court of Appeals recognized that fusion politics could have an important role in preserving this value when it struck down the fusion ban. "[R]ather than jeopardizing the integrity of the election system, consensual multiple party nomination may invigorate it by fostering more competition, participation, and representation in American politics." *McKenna,* 73 F. 3d, at 199.

5. The experience in New York with fusion politics provides considerable evidence that neither political stability nor the ultimate strength of the two major parties is truly risked by the existence of successful minor parties. More generally, "the presence of one or even two significant third parties has not led to a proliferation of parties, nor to the destruction of basic democratic institutions." Mazmanian 69; see also The Supreme Court, 1982 Term—Independent Candidates and Minority Parties, 97 Harv. L. Rev. 1, 162 (1983) ("American political stability does not depend on a two-party oligopoly. . . . [H]istorical experience in this country demontrate[s] that minor parties and independent candidacies are compatible with long-term political stability. Moreover, there is no reason to believe that eliminating restrictions on political minorities would change the basic structure of the two-party system in this country").

Index

Page references followed by t indicate tables. References followed by n indicate endnotes.

About the Authors

Gerald M. Pomper is Board of Governors Professor of Political Science at Rutgers University. The most recent of his sixteen books on American politics are *Passions and Interests* (University Press of Kansas, 1992) and *The Election of 1996* (Chatham House, 1997). Pomper has also been a visiting professor at Tel-Aviv, Oxford, and Australian National universities, and the president of his local school board.

Theodore J. Lowi has been the John L. Senior Professor of American Institutions at Cornell University since 1972. He received his doctorate at Yale in 1961. He has written or edited a dozen books, among them *The Pursuit of Justice* (with Robert F. Kennedy, 1964) and the highly influential *The End of Liberalism* (2nd ed., 1979). His 1985 book, *The Personal President: Power Invested, Promise Unfulfilled,* won the 1986 Neustadt prize for the best book published on the presidency. He is co-author of one of the leading American government texts, *American Government: Freedom and Power* (1990, 1996). His most recent books are *The End of the Republican Era* (1995) and (as co-author) *We the People* (1997).

Lowi was elected vice president of the American Political Science Association in 1985–86 and president in 1990. He served as first vice president of the International Political Science Association from 1994 to 1997 and was elected president in 1997 for a three-year term.

Joseph Romance is assistant professor of political science at Drew University. He received his B.A. from the College of William and Mary and his master's degree and Ph.D. from Rutgers University. He has published in the area of American politics, with a particular interest in American political thought and the founding era.